The Right Reverend
Doctor Benjamin Bosworth Smith,
Presiding Bishop.
From a photograph by Rockwood, New York.

The Right Reverend
Doctor Benjamin Bosworth Smith,
Presiding Bishop

From a photograph by Rockwood, New York

Reminiscences

of

Bishops and Archbishops

By

Henry Codman Potter

Bishop of New York

———

Illustrated

———

G. P. Putnam's Sons
New York and London
The Knickerbocker Press
1906

COPYRIGHT, 1906
BY
HENRY CODMAN POTTER

The Knickerbocker Press, New York

PREFACE

IN Lord Acton's Letters to Mary Gladstone there occur two suggestive sentences: "But this is true: history does not stand or fall with historians. From the thirteenth century we rely much more on letters than on histories written for the public."[1] "You have an excellent idea about those letters.[2] If you go on and arrange them, it will be very precious to him some idle day, if that should ever come, and to you all. *The inner reality of history is so unlike the back of the cards, and it takes so long to get at it,—which does not prevent us from disbelieving what is current as history, but makes us wish to sift it, and dig through mud to solid foundations.*"[3]

There is a very large truth here, which is susceptible of many illustrations. No one who has read any history, whether secular or

[1] *Letters of Lord Acton :* The Macmillan Company, 1904; p. 127

[2] These would seem to have been letters written to Miss Gladstone's father, the Hon. W. E. Gladstone, by men of light and leading in the political world of his time.

[3] *Ibid.*, p. 131.

ecclesiastical, can be unmindful of the way in which, from time to time, it is rewritten. First it was the work, on the one hand or the other, of strong partisans ; and it is not necessary to accuse them of dishonesty in order to demonstrate how, often quite unconsciously, they exaggerated facts which made for their own side of a critical issue, or minimised or even quite ignored those that made against them.

Next to these come the historians who, out of the rubbish, or the hiding-places, of history, disinter those pages in it which make not only for its accuracy, but for its comprehensiveness.

And yet there remains another element, often the most interesting, and always the most valuable of all,—the element I mean of *personality*, or individuality. For history is not, if it be history of real or enduring value, the story, alone, of events, but, most of all, of men. The passionate eagerness with which we peruse legends of illustrious people,—and, indeed, often create them out of material as mythical and shadowy as the imaginings of fable—does not spring alone, nor chiefly, from that merely vulgar personal curiosity which is little better than the love of gossip. It is essentially a sound instinct which declares that you cannot know a man alone by what he did

in his supreme moments. His lighter moments
are as verily an integral part, and as actual
a revelation of him; and we have not truly
grasped and apprehended the personality of
the great leader, or ruler, or teacher, until we
know, not only his official side, but many
others; the disclosures of which, it may easily
be, are more essentially revelations of the man,
because mainly, if not utterly, unconscious.

All this was brought home to me by an experience which, I may frankly own, is largely the
occasion of this volume. On Decoration Day,
1903, as some of my readers will remember,
there was unveiled, at the south-eastern en-
trance to Central Park, in New York, the impos-
ing equestrian statue of General W. T. Sherman, wrought by Mr. Augustus St.-Gaudens.
In the evening of that day a distinguished jour-
nalist and man of letters[1] invited a few friends
to meet the sculptor, quite informally, at his
table. Most of the guests, and with them the
host, had known General Sherman in the field,
or had served with him in our great Civil War.
Naturally enough,—especially after the ladies
had left us,—the conversation took a reminiscent turn, and recalled scenes and incidents

---

[1] The Hon. Whitelaw Reid, late Ambassador to France, and, at
present, Ambassador to the Court of St. James.

connected with the life of the great soldier whom New York had sought to commemorate. It is not enough to say of the recollections which were then exchanged that they were interesting—they were a great deal more—they were illuminative; and while driving home, that night, past that stately equestrian statue, I found myself exclaiming to my companion, "What a regrettable fact it is that all the incidents we have heard to-night, or almost all of them, will disappear with those who have related them! They are all educated men who told us what they remembered of Grant, and Sherman, and Sheridan, and the rest; but they will never put it down on paper, I fear."

But, alas, I had not gone a great way in this pharisaic judgment of my fellows, when I was seized with the memory of official relations of my own with a distinguished and interesting body of men, the House of Bishops of the Episcopal Church, with which, in one way or another, I had been connected for nearly forty years; and with the members of which for nearly half of that time my relations, both personal and official, had been especially intimate and unreserved. The histories of many of these men have already been written; and I gladly own my indebtedness to them. But that personal note, to which I have already referred, has not always been conspicuous in them; and in some cases has never been recognised.

And in this fact must be found the explanation of the Reminiscences which follow. In no sense do they presume to be biographies. In no light can they be read as embodying the graver material of history. But they will furnish some of those side-lights by means of which *individuality* in human portraiture may be detected; and in the often lighter and more playful quality of which are recognised or recalled those more endearing characteristics which make men widely remembered and genuinely beloved.

H. C. P.

NEW YORK,
December 1, 1905.

CONTENTS

ILLUSTRATIONS

Bishop Smith

I

𝔅𝔦𝔰𝔥𝔬𝔭 𝔖𝔪𝔦𝔱𝔥

HOUSE OF BISHOPS, WITH THE RIGHT REVEREND
BENJAMIN BOSWORTH SMITH, PRESIDING
BISHOP

IT was a lovely morning in October, in the
year 1866, when our good Cunarder felt
her way up the Narrows into the harbour of
New York. An American is not slow to be
proud of many things that distinguish his
country ; but among them all, few match the
charm of an American autumn. Its splendours broke on us as, in the early morning, we
climbed to the deck of our ship, and caught, as
we looked toward Staten Island, the colours of
the autumnal foliage. One remembered that
British army officer who, taken to West Point,
on an October day, by an enthusiastic American woman who lived across the river, and
led by her eager feet to a point on the shore
where he could look up and down upon the
flaming splendours of the maples that saluted
him, was asked, at length, how the scene

3

struck him, and who, after a moment's pause, answered dryly, " Pretty, but a trifle gaudy " ! One remembered him, I say,—and, in the benignity born of the incomparable environment, forgave him!

Even the Captain — it was Cooke, the austere, the frigidly reserved—was melted a little by the exquisite beauty of the scene, and offered me, condescendingly, the morning papers, which the pilot had brought on board. One returning to the confinement and drudgery of tasks from which, often, the only relief is to flee beyond seas, is not apt to be eager to search the columns of metropolitan journalism; and I, who then lived in Boston, and had that fine sense of superiority which is born alone of living in Boston, did not scan these sheets with especial interest. But suddenly my eye was caught by an announcement that a valued friend who, in the Theological Seminary of Virginia, had been my fellow-student, was that morning, in St. John's Chapel, New York, to be consecrated a missionary bishop for China. In a moment my resolution was taken to be present, if it should be possible, at this service; and, fortunately, I was able to do so. When I entered the church, the right reverend preacher (I grieve to say that I cannot

now recall him or his discourse) had just begun his sermon ; and as I glanced over the
rather meagre congregation, I realised how
scanty an interest the occasion had awakened,
even among Churchmen, in the metropolitan
city.   The sermon being ended, the bishop-
elect was presented and consecrated ; and
then followed the celebration of the Holy
Communion.

At this point there occurred an incident
which, as it has very directly to do with these
reminiscences, I cannot refrain from mention-
ing.   The bishops and other officiating clergy
had communed, and such of the congregation
as desired to do so had followed them to the
chancel rail.   At this point the late Bishop of
Connecticut (the Right Rev. Dr. John Williams) walked across the chancel to where my
predecessor, Bishop Horatio Potter, was standing, pointed towards the pew, in a side aisle, in
which I was seated, and whispered in Bishop
Potter's ear.   The latter turned, looked towards
me, nodded his head, and immediately left the
chancel, passed into a vestibule adjoining it,
and thence into the body of the church.   Advancing (in his episcopal robes, be it remembered !) down the aisle to the door of the
pew in which I was kneeling, he leaned his

elbow on the door, and, bending over, said,
" Henry, how would you like to be secretary
of the House of Bishops?"   I mention the incident as furnishing a reminder of the great
change for the better which, since then, has
come to pass in the matter of appropriate
usages in church.   Bishop Horatio Potter was
an exceptionally devout man, and distinguished
by unusual reverence in his bearing, in any
sacred edifice.   And yet, what he did was
utterly unremarked, then, while now it would
be thought impossible for any bishop to do
anything of the sort.

The situation in the House of Bishops at
that time was peculiar.   The clergyman who
had been its secretary had removed to a
foreign country and had accepted, there, a cure
of considerable dignity and importance, but had
not resigned his office as secretary of the
House of Bishops.   He had cherished the idea
of retaining this office, it was said, in the hope
of binding, thus, together, two peoples of a
common lineage and a common speech.   But
whatever his hope or purpose, the House of
Bishops did not concur with him in his view
of the conditions under which he might retain
his office as its secretary, and promptly declared that office vacant.   The unexpected-

ness of the emergency ; the necessity for some immediate provision to meet it ; the chance presence of a youth who was as likely as anybody else to be an inoffensive secretary, must, I presume, explain what followed : I was elected by a *viva voce* vote, and, I believe, *nemine contradicente,* and thus entered upon an office for which I had not had the slightest training, and in which I had not had even the most meagre experience.

That I assumed it without trepidation would be a wildly inaccurate statement of the fact. In truth, I was terrified beyond measure at the proportions of a task for which I had so little fitness, and that I was able to discharge it at all was owing, from the outset, to a courtesy and forbearance on the part of its presiding officers, and one other, of which, later, I may appropriately speak ; and which, most surely, I can never forget.

The presiding officer of the House of Bishops when, in 1866, I became its secretary, was the Right Reverend John Henry Hopkins, D.D., Bishop of Vermont. The rule which at the time determined the occupancy of the office was seniority of consecration. Bishop Hopkins had been consecrated in the year 1832 ; and there was no surviving bishop

the date of whose consecration was earlier than
his own. He was an Irishman, born in Dublin, and his earlier years had been spent
at the bar. While a layman, connected with
Trinity Church, Pittsburg, he acted during
an *interregnum* in the rectorship as a lay
reader, was elected while a layman as rector
of the parish, was ordained deacon and priest,
by Bishop White, and thus became rector of
Trinity Church, Pittsburg, where, though he
had long left it, he was, when I went to
Western Pennsylvania, vividly remembered.
He was the first bishop of his day who ventured to wear a beard, and it illustrates, very
impressively, the enormous tyranny of usage,
that, though no one denied that a beard was
given to man to be worn, and that it was a
real protection to one whose duties exposed
him to the severe winters of Vermont, Bishop
Hopkins, though ecclesiastically conservative,
was regarded as offensively eccentric, if not
theologically unsound, because he wore one !
This last imputation was made the more
swiftly because the bishop, in the construction
of his episcopal robes, had abandoned the
lawn and ruffled sleeve, and had substituted
for it something at once simpler, cooler, and
less costly.

But, though Bishop Hopkins was Presiding
Bishop in 1866, and was in the chair when I
was elected secretary of the House of Bishops,
he died in 1868 ; and in the autumn of that
year, when the General Convention assembled
in New York, he had been succeeded by the
Right Rev. Benjamin Bosworth Smith, D.D.,
the Bishop of Kentucky.

Bishop Smith was, at that time, in the thirty-
sixth year of his episcopate, having been
consecrated in 1832, together with Bishops Mc-
Ilvaine and George W. Doane, as well as with
Bishop John Henry Hopkins, his immediate
predecessor in the office of Presiding Bishop.
Bishop Smith continued to serve as Presiding
Bishop until his death, in May, 1884 ; and my
own consecration in October, 1883, was, of its
kind, his last official act.

He was born in Bristol, Rhode Island, in
1794, and, having graduated at Brown University, became rector of St. Michael's Church,
Marblehead, Mass., and, two years later, removed to a rectorship in Virginia. Subsequent to this, and after holding cures in
Charlestown and Shepherdstown, Va., he removed to Middlebury, Vt., and from thence,
after a brief ministry in Philadelphia, to Lexington, Ky., where, in 1830, he became rector

of Christ Church. Two years later he was
chosen and consecrated Bishop of Kentucky.
From this it will be seen that, as people were
classified in those days, he was a Northern
man called to exercise his episcopate in the
South in what was then a slave-holding community. His episcopate spanned, also, a
period when, from causes then fiercely oper-
ative, but now, happily, no longer existing,
Churchmen were divided, whether Northerners
or Southerners, into two schools, equally an-
tagonistic and contemptuous. The one claimed
piety, simplicity, and scriptural authority as its
distinguishing notes ; and the other glorified
order, reverence, and apostolic tradition as its
pre-eminent distinctions ; and neither willingly
lost an opportunity of disparaging brethren of
the same household of faith, with whom they
were proud to disagree.

It can readily be understood that such a
situation did not contribute to the happiness
of a bishop whose see included both these dis-
cordant elements. If he favoured one of them,
he was denounced as a partisan ; and if he
favoured neither he was reviled as a "trim-
mer." Bishop Smith was a man of peace,
gentle, tolerant, forbearing ; and a very eminent divine, long ago gone to his reward, told

me that, at a time when bowing at the name of Jesus in the Creed was considered as the note of an extreme school in the Church, Bishop Smith might be observed in churches in his diocese where such a usage prevailed to be in a state of gentle oscillation at the beginning of the Creed, to be increasingly so as the second article of it was reached, and, thereafter, gradually to relapse into a stationary position. I never believed this story, though it had in it a mark of delicate consideration for the feelings of others which one could well understand.

And indeed, in this kindlier aspect of it, it was eminently characteristic. The House over which Bishop Smith presided contained "many men of many minds"; and among them were those from whom Bishop Smith strongly and conscientiously differed. But I never saw, in his bearing or action toward them, as a presiding officer, anything but the most absolute courtesy and equity. In his theological and ecclesiastical views, he was, undoubtedly, during the whole period of his office as chairman of the House, in a minority. But in his recognition of those who rose to speak, and, most of all, in his appointment of committees, he was invariably just and generous. As he advanced in years, the task of making such

appointments became to him somewhat oner-
ous, and I was in the habit, with the unconscious audacity of youth, of writing out the
names of bishops for appointment upon special
committees, and passing them up to his desk.
He always announced them with unquestion-
ing promptness; and it was not until he was
succeeded by a bishop of a very different temper, when my committee list was on one occasion returned to me with a sharp "Will not do,
at all!" that I learned how great my presumption had been.

Bishop Smith, having been accorded an assistant for the work of the episcopate in the
Diocese of Kentucky, came to live in New
York during his closing years, and when I
rose from my knees after having knelt to receive from his hands my episcopal commission,
he closed the ordinal from which he had been
reading the words of consecration, and handed
it to me, saying, "There, Henry, you can keep
that book. I shall never use it again." And
he never did. In a few short months, his work
was ended, and he was at rest.

Bishop Whittingham

13

II

Bishop Whittingham

THE RIGHT REVEREND DR. WILLIAM ROLLINSON
WHITTINGHAM, BISHOP OF MARYLAND

ONE of the most interesting and picturesque figures in the House of Bishops
when I became its secretary was that of the
Right Reverend Dr. William Rollinson Whittingham, then the Bishop of Maryland. He
sat in the front row of the House, the seats
and desks of which were usually arranged, like
those in the United States Senate, in horse-
shoe fashion; and when I assumed the duties
of my office as secretary, my own desk or
table, raised a little above the level of the desks
of the bishops, enabled me to look down upon
the bishops in the front row. As I did so, I
observed that, while other bishops were sometimes engaged in writing letters, or in reading
them, or other papers not germane to the business of the House, Bishop Whittingham followed its procedure with close attention; and,

from time to time, made entries in a blank book before him.

Suddenly it flashed upon me that the bishop kept a record of the business of the House ; and so, after the House had adjourned for the day, I went to him with the question,

" I beg your pardon, sir, but do you keep a journal of the business of the House ? "

" Yes," replied the bishop with benignant courtesy, " such is my custom."

" May I then, sir," I ventured tremblingly to ask, " correct my minutes from yours ? "

" Most surely, my son," said the bishop, with instant perception of the situation. And from that day on, for a long time, and until I had mastered the procedure of the House, and had learned how, correctly, to keep the record of its business, I took my minutes, at the close of each day's sessions, and revised, verified, or amended them, according to this precise and unimpeachable record.

Precise and unimpeachable, I have called Bishop Whittingham's methods, and I doubt if any terms more accurately describe him. He was a man, especially in the ecclesiastical realm, not only of wide but of precise learning ; and I doubt if, when he sat in the House of Bishops, he had any superior, if he had any

The Right Reverend
Doctor William Rollinson Whittingham,
Bishop of Maryland.
From a photograph, New York.

peer, in this particular. A bishop who had quoted a pre-Reformation Archbishop of Canterbury in support of an argument he was making, was interrupted by Bishop Whittingham who said, "I beg my brother's pardon. But he quoted an Archbishop of Canterbury as having said" so and so; "did he not mean Archbishop ——?" repeating a name which, evidently, no one present recalled, but making a correction which, as obviously, no one present ventured to contradict.

But such impressive illustrations of unusual learning were accompanied by characteristics which, very often, accompany it. Bishop Whittingham had been a theological professor, and to the end he retained peculiarities not unfamiliar in such a calling. Born in New York in 1805, and graduated at the General Theological Seminary in 1825, he returned, after brief rectorships in Orange, N. J., and at St. Luke's Church, New York, to the General Theological Seminary as a professor, less than six years after his ordination to the priesthood; and though his service as a professor only extended a little more than five years, he took into the episcopate that exceptional devotion to letters and that extraordinary energy in the pursuit of ecclesiastical learning which

always distinguished him. His library was a
treasure-house of rare and choice works ; and
his acquaintance with them, happily furthered
by conditions more favourable than those of
most of his episcopal brethren, and less interrupted by the exactions of long journeys,
and frequent absences from his desk, gave
him a pre-eminence in classical, critical, and
Biblical learning, which no one ventured to
dispute.

But in the exhibition of these he was handi-
capped by characteristics at which I have already hinted. It is a law of the Church that
the testimonials, character, and qualifications
of a bishop-elect shall, before his election is
confirmed by a majority of the bishops, be
considered and discussed—if his election shall
happen to have occurred within six months
of a General Convention—in the House of
Bishops ; and, as that House sits with closed
doors, the discussions, on such occasions, are
apt to be quite informal.

It happened, on one occasion, that a recent
episcopal election had come up for review ;
and questions as to the bishop-elect were being
asked, and answered, with considerable freedom. A bishop who knew the bishop-elect in a
very intimate way was on his feet and was

being catechised, when a bishop called out,
" What kind of wife has our brother-elect ? "

" His present wife — " began the bishop
thus challenged, when the Bishop of Maryland
sprang to his feet.

" One moment ! " he cried. " Do I understand my brother aright ? Did he say ' his
present wife,' and am I to understand that,
by that phrase, he means to imply that the
brother-elect has had a previous wife ? Because, if so, I cannot vote for his confirmation.
St. Paul says ' A bishop must be the husband
of one wife,' " quoting a verse from the 1st
Epistle to Timothy[1] which scholars usually
regard as designed to forbid, in an age in
which the usage prevailed, polygamic unions.

For a moment the House, in which were a
number of bishops who, having been bereaved
of their earthly partners, had supplied their
places, sat still in stunned silence, until a prelate, whose sense of humour was as keen as
Bishop Whittingham's was feeble, rose in his
place and said, " Do I understand the Bishop
of Maryland as regarding the language of the
Apostle which he has just quoted as *mandatory ?* "

" Certainly," exclaimed Bishop Whitting-

[1] 1 Timothy iii., 2.

ham, not detecting the trap that had been laid
for him.

"Very well, then, Mr. Chairman," said the
interrogating bishop blandly; "if the Bishop
of Maryland regards the language of St. Paul,
when he says that a bishop *must be* the husband of one wife, as mandatory, I would like
to ask him what he proposes to do with the
Bishop of —— [naming a bachelor bishop]
who has n't *any?*"

There was a shout of laughter, amid which
the Bishop of Maryland flushed angrily, and
took his seat. The humour of his blunder was
wholly unperceived by him.

But the absence of these lighter qualities did
not detract from a nobility of character which
had in it features that were singularly engaging. Bishop Whittingham, like others of his
school and his traditions, had, in his earlier
episcopate, a somewhat pugnacious tenacity
for his episcopal rights and privileges. It
was said that he always insisted, at any service where it was said, on pronouncing the
Absolution. As to this there was, and I suppose still is,—though I am bound to say that I
have never encountered it,—a conviction on the
part of certain presbyters that, except in the
service of the Holy Communion, it was their

right, and not the bishop's, to pronounce the
Absolution. The matter was one, I have been
told, of sharp contention between the bishop
and a distinguished priest in his chief city,
whenever the bishop came to the church of the
latter on an episcopal visitation. But at length,
after many years of such dissension, the rector
concluded that, at best, the question was im-
material, and said so.

"You may say the Absolution, Bishop, if
you want to," he promptly remarked to the
bishop when the latter appeared in the rector's
vestry-room. "But I don't want to," exclaimed the bishop, who had, still earlier,
reached a conclusion identical with the rector's. And no one who knew him could doubt
how much that conclusion had cost him. Like
most men of great gifts, he was a person of rare
modesty; and no one who could understand
him could be ignorant how much pain it gave
him to contend for a prerogative, nor how much,
when loyalty to a principle obliged him to contend for it, to surrender it. But, as he ripened
in years, his vision expanded, rather than con-
tracted, and so it came to pass that among
those who knew him latest were those who
loved him best.

Bishop Williams

III

Bishop Williams

THE RIGHT REVEREND DR. JOHN WILLIAMS,
BISHOP OF CONNECTICUT, AND SOMETIME
PRESIDING BISHOP

THESE recollections would very inaccurately portray the life of the Episcopal
Church during the latter half of the nineteenth
century if they attempted to ignore the different schools, or indeed "parties," as one
might venture to call them, into which the
Church was divided through a large part of
that time. To do so would be to misrepresent
the history of religious opinions, during a very
interesting and critical period in American
Church history ; and to ignore influences that
have been, and will continue to be, pre-eminently potent in affecting religious beliefs.
The American mind, even farther back than
1850, had come, in the case of many thoughtful
and educated people, to realise that the English
Reformation, like most movements of its kind,
had illustrated considerable exaggeration ; and,

in throwing overboard the corruptions and tyrannies of the papacy, had, sometimes, only exchanged one form of ecclesiastical imperialism for another. It was this conviction which, after the first triumphs of Puritanism in America, produced a reaction that was impatient of an authority that intruded, often, into the domain of things ἀδιάφορα ; and that, while claiming large freedoms for conscience, for the individual disciple, only exchanged one bondage for another.

It was this that went a long way to explain the growth of the Church in Connecticut ; and which accounted for the evolution of a type of Churchmanship, there, which it must be owned, as it awakened, elsewhere, a certain envy, developed in Connecticut Churchmen a decided complacency. To be known as a "Connecticut Churchman" was to be ticketed as a person who held reverent views of authority, conservative ideas of worship, and, pre-eminently, orthodox opinions about dogma. The late Bishop of Connecticut once told me a story of his venerable predecessor, and the late Bishop of Rhode Island, which curiously illustrates this. At the time that Bishop Brownell was Bishop of Connecticut, Bishop Williams was his Assistant, and Bishop Clark—then the

The Right Reverend Doctor John Williams,
Bishop of Connecticut.

From a photograph by Hennigar Bros., Middletown, Conn.

Rev. Dr. Thomas M. Clark — was the rector
of a church in Hartford, in which city all
three happened, one Sunday morning, to be.
After morning service, Bishop Brownell and
Bishop Williams chanced to meet. Bishop
Brownell, it should be said, was born in Massachusetts, and had been reared under influences
which certainly had not dislodged earlier impressions; for, though he graduated at Union
College (in 1804), and had been tutor, lecturer,
and professor there during the presidency of
Eliphalet Nott, he had not learned, any more
than had his great preceptor, to disesteem New
England ideas of orthodoxy. In his own presidency, as first in that office at Washington (now
Trinity) College, and, later, in his episcopate,
when he was Bishop of Connecticut, Bishop
Brownell was the incarnation of traditional
orthodoxy; and unfamiliar views of truth had,
to him, a very menacing and heterodox sound.

On the occasion to which I refer, he came
in upon Bishop Williams somewhat unexpect-
edly; and the latter, not unnaturally, en-
quired, "Where have you been this morning,
Bishop?" "Down at Christ Church," answered Bishop Brownell, "where I heard Clark.
He preached pantheism; but he did n't know
it!" If Dr. Clark's sermon could be disin-

terred to-day, it is doubtful whether the most critical eye could detect in it any savour of pantheism ; but Connecticut standards in those days were both narrow and austere.

That, among Congregationalists, this was pre-eminently the case was doubtless, in part, the explanation of the step that young John Williams took when he forsook that fellowship. He was born in Deerfield, Mass., in 1817, and his ancestry was alike gifted and distinguished.

" His father " (I quote the admirable sketch of Bishop Williams by the Rev. Dr. Samuel Hart in the *Churchman* of February 18, 1899) " was Ephraim Williams, who was born in 1760, the year of the accession of George III. He was well known as a lawyer, and in public life, beginning practice as a partner of Theodore Sedgwick in Stockbridge. Through his grandmother, the bishop was also descended from the Reverend John Cotton, the first minister of Boston, and the Reverend Solomon Stoddard of Northampton. "

The bishop's mother, for many years a familiar figure in Middletown during his residence there, was Emily Trowbridge, much younger than her husband and long outliving him.

John Williams, her son, says Dr. Hart,

"was prepared for college in the academies at Deerfield and Northfield, Mass., and was entered at Harvard Col-

lege in 1831, when he had just completed his fourteenth
year. His parents had been Unitarians ; but the young
man, while at Harvard, largely owing to the influence
of the Reverend Benjamin Davis Winslow, after much
discussion and study, became, in his convictions, a
Churchman."

No fact in the life of Bishop Williams is
more interesting than this change, and the
circumstances under which it came to pass.
The atmosphere in which, as a youth at Harvard, he found himself was not merely cold,
but *dry ;* and there was in the youth an intellectual element which he never outgrew. It
was not conspicuous in his public or private
utterances, but it was revealed alike in his
reading and in his friendships ; and no one can
recall the little volume which, in 1844, he
issued from the parsonage of St. George's
Church, Schenectady, N. Y., while he was the
rector of that parish, which bore the title,
Ancient Hymns of Holy Church, and which
was dedicated to his friend the Rev. Arthur
Cleveland Coxe, "in memory," to quote his
own words, "of many conversations on the
sacred ritual of the Church of God"—no one,
I say, can recall this page in his history without recognising that, in the Church to which
he turned in his youth, and which he was to

adorn by his eminent services in its episcopate, he found, of necessity, his intellectual and spiritual home.

In that home it was no less natural that he should speedily be called to a position of large influence and of intellectual dignity. In 1848 he was chosen to be President of Trinity College, "the youngest person, it is believed," says Dr. Hart, "ever chosen to be head of a college." This is not quite true, even in contemporaneous history; for Eliphalet Nott was no older, if as old, when chosen President of Union College, and a grandson of his, whose modesty forbids my naming him, was called to the same eminence when only twenty-six years of age. But the distinction in the case of Dr. John Williams consisted in what some one has called "the curious ripeness of his youth"; and in qualities of vision and prudence, rarely found except as the notes of middle life or advanced age.

It was not surprising that the exceptional illustration of such qualities, in his brilliant career as the President of Trinity College, should have turned towards him the attention of the Diocese of Connecticut, when, in 1850, it attempted, and, in 1851, succeeded, in electing an assistant to its venerable bishop. Dr. Wil-

liams was elected by a very large majority both
of the clerical and lay votes ; was consecrated
in St. John's Church, Hartford, on October
29th, and there began an episcopate of altogether exceptional influence and power.

This was by no means because he dis-
esteemed the traditions which were behind him,
or sought to replace them with others. He
did neither. Retaining his connection with
Trinity College for some two years, he became
a year later, and remained until his death,
the head of the Berkeley Divinity School at
Middletown, Conn., of which he was not only
the founder, but, though surrounded with able
associates for nearly half a century, the supreme inspiration. It would be as interesting
as it would be impossible to catalogue the men
and ideas that he formed and disseminated ;
and though many of his pupils travelled far
afield, in the sense of any slavish adherence to
the views and view-points in which he had nurtured them, there was — there is — no one of
them whose mind will ever lose the impress of
his thought. His own intellectual activities
were so vigorous and so scholarly that he com-
pelled his students to *think;* and held them
fast to traditions whose potency, though they
were often quite unconscious of the fact,

resided largely in his own unique and attractive personality.

My own acquaintance with him began when I was a child, and he then rector of St. George's Church, Schenectady, N. Y. My father was then a professor in Union College; and Mr. Williams (as he then was) ministered in St. George's to a congregation which included a row of small boys, of whom I was one. I blush to say that I cannot recall his preaching—but those were not days in which children were considered in the Church's services, being mainly under discipline as "unruly members" of the congregation whose chief office there was to sit still. Years afterward, however, when, as a young rector, I became secretary of the House of Bishops, it was Bishop Williams who nominated me, and to him I owed much kindness and generous forbearance in connection with the earlier crudeness and manifold imperfections of my secretarial efforts.

When I took up those tasks, Bishop Williams had sat in the House of Bishops for a quarter of a century; and was one of its most commanding figures. He spoke but rarely, and briefly; but when he spoke, all men listened, and his utterances were always *ad rem*, and

exceptionally illuminating. No one, in my
experience of it, had a more accurate knowledge of the history of legislation in the House
of Bishops; and no one, as it seemed to me,
was able to deal with delicate and intricate
questions more dispassionately. Before he
ceased to have a seat in the House he had become Presiding Bishop; and in that capacity
illustrated the highest qualities of a presiding
officer. There have been chairmen of ecclesiastical bodies who constantly recalled a very
noble old divine, the Rev. Dr. Levi Bull, who
presided in the convention that elected my
father Bishop of Pennsylvania. It is told that
Dr. Bull, having on one occasion put a question to the Convention of the Diocese of Pennsylvania, and having had a loud response to
his request, " Those in favour of the resolution
will say *aye*," at once declared the resolution
carried. " But, Doctor," said a grave divine,
rising in his place, " you have n't called for the
noes ! " " Oh, well," said the doctor, " *we don't
want any noes.*" There have been chairmen and
presiding bishops in the House who recalled
Dr. Bull—though they never dispensed so cheer-
fully with the ordinary rules of deliberative
bodies ! But in Bishop Williams's case, when
he presided in the House, his regard for the

3

Rules of Order was most scrupulous; and one
never knew, unless one chose to infer it from
previous associations, utterances, or inherit-
ances, on which side of any particular question
were his personal sympathies. In a word, he
was a most impartial presiding officer; never a
partisan, never a limp creature of the impulse of
the moment; courteous, but firm; and amid
the confusions of debate often bringing order
out of chaos, by a few unimpassioned but
illuminating sentences.

In a word, this rare scholar, teacher, and
prelate united with gifts which would have
made him illustrious in any of these walks of
life others which, rarer in their moral quality,
were the pre-eminent enrichments of a noble
character. And crowning them all was a note
of Doric dignity and simplicity, which was the
fit capital of so strong and stately a column.
In an estimate of his character now some six
or seven years old, I find that I have emphasised that aspect of Bishop Williams, and I
venture to repeat it here.

" BISHOP WILLIAMS:

" HIS DIRECTNESS AND SIMPLICITY

" If I were asked to indicate what, among other things,
of which others will doubtless speak, always impressed

me, in the late Bishop of Connecticut, I should say his
directness and simplicity. I wrote him, often, in one or
other of those perplexities in which we all turned to him;
and his answer, or counsel, was always clear, candid, ex-
plicit. If he did not know, he frankly said he did not
know. If he had an opinion or conviction, he as frankly
uttered it. In a sermon, yesterday, delivered on the
birthday of the latter, I ventured to bracket him with
Lincoln—the two so unlike in their traditions and training, so often like in their unadorned and columnar
directness and simplicity. Bishop Williams's pine coffin
and plain black suit were fine notes of his impatience of
costly ornament or personal display. No more beautiful
example has been given to the Church than his modest
home, his frugal and inexpensive surroundings, his large
indifference to the decorative and the ornamental. His
learning, his rare power (the two things are by no means
identical) of imparting learning; his unwearied devotion
to the work of his great office; his tenacity of opinion,
or, rather, conviction, in matters of the Faith, coupled
with a noble charity,—I wish I could violate the privacy
of others and illustrate this,—toward those who differed
from him; his stately presence; his power in the pulpit;
his influence over men,—all these the Church has large
reason gratefully to remember. But not less, in an age
over-given to ostentation, tawdriness, and mere orna-
mentation in men's worship and persons, has it reason to
hold in grateful memory the consistent example which
he gave us all of masculine and dignified simplicity."

These reminiscences would be incomplete if
I did not enrich them with the memories of
pupils of Bishop Williams; and two of them

have given me some *memorabilia* of their college or seminary days. The first of these is from the pen of the Rev. Horace B. Hitchings, D.D., a graduate of Trinity College, and later a presbyter in the Diocese of New York.

"You honour me greatly in asking for reminiscences of the late Bishop Williams for your forthcoming book. You little know, however, how great a favour you ask. My remembrances of that great and good man are among my most sacred treasures, and it seems almost profane to write any of them out for other eyes to see, or other minds to know.

"For some reason incomprehensible to me, the bishop allowed me to come in close contact with himself; and after a time the relationship was more in the nature of confident and loving friendship, than of teacher and pupil, or of bishop and priest. The intimacy, however, was never of the sort that breeds contempt. The closer it became, and the more I learned of the character and disposition and aspirations of the man, the greater, and nobler, and holier, he seemed to be.

"Never shall I forget the first time I met the bishop face to face. I was but a boy, just entering Trinity College, of which he was president. A room had been assigned me. A perfect stranger to both students and professors, in loneliness and heart-heavy with homesickness, I was arranging the little furniture I possessed to make it comfortable. A rap came upon the door. I was alarmed, and having heard much of the trying scenes a freshman was expected to go through, I supposed my time had come. I opened the door cautiously, and to my great astonishment there stood the president. I know not

which possessed me most, awe or fear. What breach of
college discipline had I been guilty of, that the president
should be after me, so soon? I never dreamed that he
had come to make a friendly call; but never shall I forget the kind words he spoke, nor with what interest he
asked after my comfort. Surely I could no longer feel
a stranger or lonely, for I was certain of a friend in no
less a person than the president himself. Those kind
words warmed my heart, and filled me with a love that
made college life a delight, and has caused it ever since
to be a memory most sweet to look back upon.

"It is hardly proper, perhaps, to relate the incidents
of college life. The frolics and pranks of students are
trifling and foolish enough, at best, but from some of
them the character and good heart of our president was
made manifest. He never forgot that he had once been
a boy. That, I believe, was the secret of his successful
management of the college; and of his extraordinary
influence over young men, even in his advancing years.

"It was the custom of those in authority to sell the
grass on the *campus* to some farmer in the neighbourhood.
It was also the custom of the students to destroy as
much of the hay made from it as was possible, usually
by setting it on fire. On one occasion a trusting and
confiding farmer left a load of hay on his cart to stand
on the *campus* over night. A great opportunity was
open for the students to have fun. The president was
certain advantage would be taken of it, and so watched
to see what would be done with the hay. He had a cap
and suit of clothes much like those the students wore.
These he donned, and waited patiently among the trees
in the grove. About eleven at night, the students—
some of the mischievous ones—began to gather. The

night was dark, it was quite impossible to recognise friends from foes, so the president joined the crowd. It was the intention of the students to dump the hay, cart and all, into the river running in the rear of the college grounds, and thus give the hay a dose of water instead of fire, as it had been strictly forbidden them to do. The president followed in the rear, and just as the edge of the bank was reached and they were about to let go the cart, in his natural voice he said, 'Come, boys, I guess we have hauled this hay far enough. Let us go to our rooms.' Such a scattering as there was of the boys was never seen before on college grounds ; and such fear and trembling as there was among some of the students the next day will be long remembered by them. That was the last of it, however ; no student was called up or disciplined. The suspense, the fear and trembling for hours was punishment enough. But the incident, and treatment of it, won the hearts and respect of the students for the president ever after.

"On another occasion a different phase of the president's character was brought out when the hay was put in the college chapel, thus making the chapel unfit for use at the hour of morning prayer. Not a word was said about the matter during the day, no inquiries were made as to who did the mischief. A dead and dreaded silence was observed. The chapel was cleared out, and cleaned up. The students assembled as usual for evening prayers. The president, though contrary to his custom, officiated. Before commencing the service, however, he addressed the students in tones full of sorrow, and told how pained he was to find there were any present who had so little respect for that sacred place as to desecrate it in the manner in which it was desecrated the night before. He did not know, and did not want to know who the guilty ones were, but trusted the act was one of thoughtless levity, rather than a deliberate act of sacrilege. ' The Lord is in His Holy Temple ; let all the earth keep silence before Him.' There was not a student present, whether guilty or not, whose soul was not touched by the president's tone and reverent words, and who was not heartily ashamed of the thoughtless prank. I doubt whether any college chapel service was ever joined in by the whole body of students more earnestly and devoutly than was that evening prayer. A solemn stillness and holy awe seemed to pervade the place, and mark it indeed as a sacred spot. It is needless to say the chapel was ever after unmolested.

"On one occasion the president told me he was sitting at his window during a heavy thunder-storm. The rain came down in torrents. Great was his surprise to see a student, one of the model students at that, bareheaded and in his dressing-gown and slippers, running across the *campus* with a water pitcher in his hand. What can the boy be up to? he thought. He watched, and saw him climb to the top of a low building near by, empty his water pitcher, and run back again. What did it all mean After the storm was over Professor B., who was making observations of the fall of rain for the United States Weather Bureau, came to the president's room and reported the greatest fall of water of which he had ever heard. ' I have searched the records for years back. There was nothing ever like it. So many inches of water in so many minutes.' The secret of the student's water pitcher was out; but the president kept his counsel. 'Professor, I think I would not make an official report of this storm until I had looked into the matter more thoroughly. There must be some mistake about it. Are you sure there is no leakage from the roof or elsewhere that would affect the water gauge?' The president sent for the student to come to his room. 'John, you are neither a duck nor a goose, so don't go out in the rain again with a pitcher of water. You might seriously interfere with the calculations of the United States Weather Bureau.' John afterwards became a distinguished bishop in the Church, but, so far as heard from, was never known either to deny, or affirm, the truth of the story.

"As students, we all loved the president, respected and obeyed him. His kind heart and extraordinary tact in dealing with the various cases of discipline that made it necessary for him to act—and act with severity sometimes—won our approval. No delinquent stood in his presence who did not feel that he would be dealt with justly and wisely. Naughty boys know when they are naughty and deserve punishment; and so long as the punishment is commensurate with the offence, and is administered in love, and not in anger, the sentence of punishment is acquiesced in, and the discipline endured without a murmur.

"I well remember, on a certain night as I was going to my room rather late, meeting in the grove a student, who afterwards became distinguished as an eloquent orator, a powerful politician, and eminent governor. He was in the dumps, in rather a repentant mood, and lashing himself with stripes. 'What is the matter?' I asked. 'What have you been up to?' 'Oh, nothing, only getting a horse into one of the recitation-rooms on the ground floor. The prex caught me at it. He's always around, night and day. You can't get rid of him. Now, to-morrow he 'll have me up, and talk to me kindly as he always does. Oh, how I dread it.' Then, passing sentence on himself, he said: 'I shall be rusticated again, sent away to some stupid country place, to pass a month with some more stupid country parson.' All of which happened.

"It was the custom of the president to visit the students in their rooms from time to time; and there was no occasion looked forward to by them with greater delight. His conversation during these visits was interesting, instructive, and amusing. He had a fund of stories to illustrate and illuminate his talk; and one could not but marvel at the aptness with which they were applied. As a story-teller it is questionable if he ever had his superior.

"The simplest events of his life, full of queer incidents, would be told in language so forcible and ofttimes so funny as to make them gems of a story, and set his listeners splitting with laughter. But there were events out of which came grave stories as well as gay, which not infrequently would bring tears to the eyes. He rarely ever repeated a story, and somehow his stories never seemed out of place, so perfectly did they fit in with the conversation and occasion.

"I remember once, one of the students, more bold than the others, took the liberty to say: 'I can't believe such a thing ever happened. I think you must have made up that story as you went along to illustrate what you are talking about.' The president laughed, with a mischievous twinkle in his eyes, as much as to say, 'You have found me out in part, at least.'

"There was a time of great excitement in the college when our president was being voted for as Bishop of New

York, but of great rejoicing in a few days after when he
was actually elected Bishop of Connecticut. The college
buildings were illuminated, he was welcomed home by
the whole body of students with speeches and hurrahs
and a band of music. But alas, how little we thought, on
that night of joy, that we were making merry over what
was to become to us a cause of deep sorrow. To be made
Bishop of the Diocese necessarily took him away from
the college as president, and eventually from Hartford
as a resident. We missed his wise counsel and kind care,
and deeply mourned his absence. Some of the students,
however, myself among the number, after graduation
followed the bishop to his new home at Middletown and
became students in theology, and right glad were we to
come once again under his instruction. We were older
then, more mature in judgment, and could fully appreciate the great learning and ripe scholarship of the bishop.
There seemed to be no department in theology of
which he was not master. Scriptural exegesis, ecclesiastical history, doctrinal theology, whether of the ancient
fathers, or modern writers, of all schools and shades of
opinion, he seemed to know all about. With the con-
troversy of the Roman Church, as it came up during the
Reformation period, as well as the claims and discussions of the dissenters in after years, he was quite
familiar. Hebrew, Greek, and Latin were all the same
to him, and it made but little difference whether he read
the Scriptures in one or the other tongue. But the
bishop did not confine his studies to theology. He was
a great and rapid reader of almost every kind of literature, even novels. He had a wonderfully retentive
memory. He seemed never to forget anything he had
ever read: and years afterwards could repeat it over
almost word for word.

"I remember on one occasion being in his study, when a celebrated doctor of divinity, a great connoisseur in old books, came in, much elated that he had procured, after years of waiting, an old book of poetry. He had sent to London for it, seeing it advertised in a sale of rare books. 'I do not believe there is another copy of this book in the United States,' he said. The bishop was silent for a moment, as if in deep thought, then replied, 'Is that the poet who wrote this?' and repeated several verses, and then again repeated from another poem. 'Why, yes,' said the doctor, 'but how did you know this poetry?' 'Well, I have not opened the book for twenty years, I think, but there is a copy of it on the top shelf of my bookcase.' The good doctor was much amazed. 'How could you remember the poetry after all these years, and why did I never find out you had the book?'

"The bishop's mind always impressed me as being an orderly arranged storehouse, where every package of knowledge was labelled and could be taken down and used at will. His power of concentration of thought was remarkable. No conversation or noise seemed to distract or disconcert him in the least, whether reading or writing. Many times when several persons were in his study talking, and the bishop was sitting at his desk writing, I have heard them say, 'We had better go elsewhere; we shall disturb the bishop.' 'Oh, no, stay and go on with your talk. You don't bother me at all.' And the result of his writing would ofttimes be one of his able sermons, or a learned article for some newspaper or magazine.

"During the trying times of the Civil War, the bishop was now and then obliged to do things which doubtless caused him much pain, and went greatly against his kind heart. On one occasion he was standing on the steps of his residence with his mother and friends viewing a company of soldiers marching off to the front. A young man, whose father had been a distinguished officer under the United States Government, but had chosen to cast in his lot with the South, and with whom the bishop had been on intimate and friendly terms, approached and stretched out his hand for a cordial greeting, at the same time making some sneering remark about the passing soldiers. The bishop, putting both hands behind him, drew back with a severe frown on his face. In sharp, severe tones, he said: ' I will not shake hands with one who is a traitor to his country and who speaks contemptuously of those going forth to defend its flag.' The young man turned away rebuked, much abashed and doubtless very angry, but it was 'a time to speak,' and the bishop spoke in language not to be misunderstood.

"One of the pleasantest and most delightful remembrances of the bishop is the affection he had for his mother, and the kind and considerate care he always took for her comfort and happiness. In her declining years, when age and sickness confined her to her room, he really made that room his study, moving there his writing-desk and some of his choicest books. It was a long sickness, not painful, but rather a gradual wearing out of the system incident to old age. Many pleasant evenings do I recall spent in that room of sickness; and never can one who was present forget the day on which that noble and good woman died. It was the day of the annual ordination of the graduating class of the Berkeley Divinity School. Of course the bishop must be present to ordain, but his mother was dying and he could not leave her bedside. It was arranged that he was not to attend the service but to be notified when the time came for the act of ordination. Before it came, however, while the service, was in progress, the spirit of his mother departed, and the bishop, almost broken-hearted, bowed down with grief, hastened to the church, stepped into the chancel, and knelt at the altar. All knew the great sorrow of his life was upon him ; and every heart present beat in loving sympathy, a sharer of his anguish.

"It was my great privilege to accompany the bishop on many of his visitations over the diocese. The most cordial greeting awaited him everywhere. Men and women, as well as children, gathered about him for a kind word and a warm pressure of his generous hand. Of course the church was always crowded with hearers. Every parishioner made it a point to be present on the bishop's visit to the parish. His sermons during the early years of his bishopric were usually written and delivered from manuscripts, but in later years were always extemporaneous. His addresses to the candidates for confirmation were most sympathetic and touching, full of wise counsel and encouragement, breathing only the spirit of Christian love and charity, and making the candidates feel that they were welcome to their Father's house and to the service of their Divine Lord and Master.

"On one occasion in a country parish, at an early evening service, I remember the lights suddenly went out soon after the bishop commenced his discourse. It was a written sermon, but with no hesitation or apparent embarrassment the bishop went on, and in the dim twilight, growing each minute darker, delivered one of the most eloquent sermons I ever heard him preach. The

senior warden of the parish, a noble old sea captain, a
devout Churchman, and a godly man, grandfather, I believe, to one of our present distinguished bishops, sat
near the front row of seats. He became so enraptured
and enthusiastic over the bishop's eloquence that he
would every little while forget himself, and nudging
his good wife, who sat by his side, would exclaim in
tones so loud as to be distinctly heard in the chancel,
'Good! Good!'

"I said to the bishop after the service: 'It was so dark
you could not possibly see to read; how could you remember your sermon to deliver it so readily?' 'Why,
bless you, I did not deliver the written sermon at all. I
could not see a word. I gradually drifted into what
I said, but I hope it was all right.' 'Never was there a
better sermon,' I said. This shows how quick and ready
the bishop was to overcome difficulties, and master the
situation. He never seemed at a loss what to do, and
he always seemed to do just the right thing. He
was 'apt and meet' in a most extraordinary sense of
those words.

"It would be a very incomplete account of the bishop
if I should leave unmentioned his bodily presence.
While it might be said of him as was said of St. Paul,
'his letters are weighty and powerful,' it could not
be said 'his bodily presence is weak and his speech
contemptible.' The bishop was what would be called a
handsome man. Manly and noble in every feature, tall
and graceful in every movement, it always seemed to
me the description of Saul would well apply to him:
'a choice young man, and there was not among the
children of Israel a goodlier person than he. When he
stood among the people he was higher than any of the

people from his shoulders and upward.' The standard portrait of the bishop, by Church, gives a correct impression of his personal presence, and the likeness is perfect. I always remember what one of my vestrymen said to me after a visitation of the bishop to the parish: 'He reminds me of a king; his presence is royal, and he delivers his sermons as one speaking with authority.' Of course there is much more that might be said of the bishop and much better said. My memory is full of interesting incidents. I have selected such matter, however, as I conclude others will consider too trivial to mention, and which I fear, now it is down in black and white, and looked at with cold and critical eyes, may belittle the great man's noble character, rather than give it its true expression. But is it not, after all, the small and apparently unimportant things of life, the every-day occasions, and the manner of dealing with them, that make a man's character great and good? It is easy enough to be magnanimous on exceptional occasions when the eyes of the world are upon you, but it is not always easy to 'deal justly and love mercy' and act wisely in the small and ofttimes annoying events of the passing hour. Truly he is more than an ordinary man who is great to his valet, and to those nearest him; but I think one can say without question that Bishop Williams was a greater and better man to those closest to him than he was to those who saw and knew him only in his public and official capacity.

" Before closing, let me say what was once said to me of the bishop, by one who knew him well, but who was not of the same faith—by one too who was fitted as few others to judge correctly of his learning, and literary ability, and of his oratorical powers.

"The Rev. Dr. John Lord, famous as a lecturer and powerful as a delineator of character, said: 'Had the bishop become a lawyer instead of a clergyman, he would have been one of the ablest lawyers and judges the country has ever seen; logical and convincing in argument, just, and discerning truth from error in his conclusions.'"

To these interesting reminiscences of college life, I may fitly add those which follow, from the present Bishop of California, the Right Reverend William F. Nichols, D.D. Bishop Nichols, like Dr. Hitchings, enjoyed in a rare degree the confidence of Bishop Williams; and the relations of the two men grew increasingly intimate, until, on different shores of the Western Hemisphere, they came to bear the same episcopal yoke. In this point of view there is a subtone of pathos in the recollections, from the pen of Bishop Nichols, which follow:

"Bishop Williams's boyhood was spent at historic old Deerfield, in Massachusetts; and sometimes, when in a reminiscent mood, he would absorb his listeners in his early memories of home and of that country and community. A charm of the experiences that he recalled was that they were illustrations of a type of early New England family and town life that has now been almost entirely changed. Evenings there were around the hearth-stone, the family thrown upon its own resources for passing the long winters, when tales were told of the days of the Indian savagery, and traditions of stirring scenes at Deerfield itself were handed down at the chimney-side. These made a great impression upon the boy John Williams, kinsmen of his family having suffered, among them the Rev. John Williams, who was carried away into Canada. This may in part account for the bishop's life-long fondness for Walter Scott's tales, which he heard as they came out and were read in that same family circle. It was the bishop's wont often to turn from the cares of his official station, in those evenings in his Middletown home, to his Scott's novels; and it was a happy choice when, Bishop Williams having provided that, after his death, his close friend, Bishop Doane, of Albany, should select any souvenir he wished from the Middletown house, that well-used set passed to one who could appreciate their associations so truly. And Whittier's *Snow-bound* ever seemed especially to appeal to Bishop Williams's memories, as

> ' Shut in from all the world without
> We sat the clean-winged hearth about.'

When the first snow-storm of a winter came, he liked to read aloud that poem, or quote from it, as he looked out upon the falling flakes, the lines:

> ' As zigzag wavering to and fro
> Crossed and recrossed the wingèd snow, '

noting with almost boyish glee—' See how true that is,— the flakes never seem to alight anywhere! ' One memory impressed upon him, as he used to say, by its conse- quences to him from a paternal source, as well as by

4

the experience itself, carries us into the meeting-house atmosphere of the day—for his boyhood was not spent in the Church of his after choice. Many a long Sunday hour he spent in one of the old-time square pews, sitting through the old-time discourse, before which it is to be feared sometimes the hour glass had about the only signs of real 'following.' It so happened that directly in front of the boy John Williams sat a worthy magnate of that congregation, whose queue so adjusted itself to that gentleman's habitual slumbers in sermon time that, as his head slipped down on the back of the pew, the queue took an angle upward and projected over into the pew of the Williams family with a sort of weekly challenge to the boy, not so absorbed in the current sermon as to be oblivious of the fact. Sunday after Sunday the temptation came, and was resisted; but it finally became too much for the boy nature; and in a moment when, both in his own and the adjoining pew, somnolence seemed to reign, the challenge was met; the queue was firmly clutched and tweaked, with an instantaneous effect upon several staid family pews in that immediate vicinity; and the boy never forgot it!

"Like the queue itself, such experiences are now of the long past; and the very image of that family life under the conditions of the hearth-stone, and with the survivals of the older New England, carries one back to some of the best stock, as it does to some of the most wholesome and interesting traits, in our American origins.

"And to that striking filial trait of Bishop Williams which one recalls in his tender care for his aged mother, so stately and queenlike, as she made her home with him until her death in 1872,—not to speak of love of home amid all the home-leavings of his busy almost

half-century bishop's life, nor of his allegiance to the
best of old New England traditions and ways,—how he
enjoyed such a book as Mrs. Stowe's *Old Town Stories*,
with its Parson Lothrop and Sam Lawson! He would
never have any new-fangled electricity about him if
he could help it,—how much that Deerfield boyhood
explains it all. And, like Bishop Huntington, there was
never any country to him quite equal to the New England hills and vales.

"His college days, first at Harvard, then at Trinity,
won for him the high respect of his contemporaries, as,
for example, in the tribute paid him some years since in
a book of voluble reminiscences written by one of his
Trinity classmates, Robert Tomes. The late Roman
Catholic Archbishop of Baltimore, James Roosevelt
Bayley, was a classmate and roommate of Bishop Williams at Trinity. The well-known Josiah Quincy was
President of Harvard while John Williams was an undergraduate there; and the bishop had some memories
of his experiences there, and anecdotes of President
Quincy, which showed how the gentle touch of the
higher human in the sedate president appealed to the
like characteristic of the undergraduate. In Dr. Williams's own presidency of Trinity this same quality was
reproduced, as on one occasion when he had called
before him an irrepressible student to reprimand him.
The young man gave a mischievous turn to his explanation, which so touched the keen sense of the ludicrous
of the president that, in sheer protection of his gravity,
he was obliged to cover his explosion of laughter by an
instant and most severe, ' Leave the room, sir, this minute! ' Is there any wonder that he always won the love
of his students ?

"And his episcopate was itself so full of things to be

remembered that the earlier data of his college days have been in a background which has receded with the living memories of his then contemporaries, who have almost, if not quite, passed from earth. Indeed, so varied and so strongly impressed are the reminiscences of him all over the Church, that his episcopate has had the rare distinction, like that of Bishop Samuel Wilberforce, of becoming a sort of residuary legatee of all episcopal experiences and stories that are unidentified with any other name, whether Bishop Williams had anything to do with them or not. But any one who ever knew him is well aware that in well-authenticated sayings, and stories, and experiences, his episcopate was so rich and delightful, and altogether notable, that any one who attempts to recall them finds it hopeless to do any justice to them in any off-hand way, and has a new sense of the greater pity it is that he could not himself have gathered them up in some autobiographical way or that some competent hand could not have systematically compiled his memoirs. Such sayings as ' The Puritans first fell on their own knees, then on the aborigines,' or his quiet rebuke at a dinner when some one was pressing him rather too inquisitively about the affairs of one of his clergy with some such question as: ' Has the Rev. Mr. —— said anything to you about——?' ' Nothing *to speak of*, sir,' will long be quoted from his lips. And whatever any one may find coming to his mind, first, out of a multitude of memories, it will be inevitable that some other memory of him that some one else could tell ought not to be overlooked in any fair recollection of the inexhaustible material that Bishop Williams has left. But even if they chiefly betray the slightness of the sketch, two or three memoranda may be added, taken somewhat at random.

" On one of his visitations, the bishop found himself, in the time between breakfast and the Sunday morning service, alone with the rector's young hopeful in the study. Chummy relations were at once established, and the little four-year-old said: ' Oh, Bishop, would n't you like to have me show you my picture-book?' ' Of course I would,' said the bishop. Thereupon the book was brought out and looked over in detail with full zest by both bishop and child. When the sitting was about to adjourn the little fellow intensely delighted the bishop by remarking: ' Now, Bishop, don't tell papa about this, 'cause he won't let me look at this book on Sunday!'

" All students of the Berkeley Divinity School of a generation ago will remember ' Tim,' the faithful janitor, —so faithful that, when told to do anything, he showed a charming indifference to any after circumstances which might be supposed to modify directions,—any ' law of the conditioned,' for Tim was no metaphysician. Now it so happened, one morning, when the bishop was attending the chapel services that his good housekeeper, thinking he was in his library, asked Tim to get from him certain keys she wished to use. Tim obediently started out. Going to the library, and not finding the bishop there, he soon learned of the chapel service, and proceeded forthwith to the principal chapel door, which is on the ' Quad ' side. Just as Tim opened the door, the epistoler had announced, ' Here endeth the epistle.' The bishop was the gospeller, but before he could make the customary announcement, in that Divinity School chapel of punctilious rubrical propriety, was heard from the side door, in riotous, if unconscious innovation by our good Roman brother Tim, ' If you please, sir, Miss T——wants the keys.' ' Very well, you go into the house and get them. The——is written in the ——'

came back from the bishop in his place with all unruffled
rubrical order and readiness, and with that dignity that
ever characterised Bishop Williams in service and out.

"One of the bishop's private secretaries once called
his attention to a facetious statement in a newspaper to
the effect that they were proposing to put a tax on bachelors,—the bishop having never married. 'Read it,' said
the bishop. The secretary then read it in full, to the
effect that upon young bachelors the tax was to be light,
but as years increased and probabilities of change dimin-
ished the tax was to be made more and more weighty,
until to those upwards of seventy—as the bishop then
was—it was to amount to some hundreds of dollars an-
nually. The secretary read the latter part with something of a gusto. When he had finished, the bishop
said, calling the secretary by name, 'P——, it comes
high, but it 's worth it.'

"Such kindly flashes of humour, in sometimes a mock
heroic tone, were only the sparks thrown off from the
strong voltage of his great life current. It was a current which carried men along with him. Its momentum
lasts still in many a ministry, and now with statistical accuracy it could be said in many an episcopate. That
strong, quiet dynamic energy of his character and work
has been interpreted into action in the Church, as has
happened in the case of our modern leaders. But it
would not be easy to describe it even in a full memoir.
And here we only catch some of the scintillations of its
presence, as in the night the wheels of a modern motor
now and then sparkle and crackle with the subtle power
that is all the while mightily turning them onward."

When Bishop Williams died, there appeared
a number of tributes to his memory, and among

them the lines with which this paper concludes. The writer, the late Rev. Robert Clarkson Tongue, was then—or had lately been—a pupil of Bishop Williams' in the Berkeley Divinity School, and was at the time of his death a rector in the Diocese of Connecticut. They are singularly happy in describing a species of influence in exerting which the fourth Bishop of Connecticut was undoubtedly pre-eminent.

" Saint of Northumbria! Well may England prize
   Her priestly scholar and revere his name;
   The long millennium doth not dim the eyes
   Of those whose lamps are kindled at his flame.
   First of a dynasty that has no end,
   This is the teacher's heritage, to mark
   The lives of men unborn, and so to send
   His ageless purpose gleaming down the dark.

" New England Bæda, thou of yesterday,
   The years are all before thee. Year on year
   Shall speed thy purpose on its widening way,
   When we are dust who looked upon thy bier.
   We bear thine impress, we are of thy line,
   And we shall be forgot; the torch we hold
   Was of thy lighting, that more clear shall shine
   After the long millennium is told."

Bishop Eastburn

IV

Bishop Eastburn

THE RIGHT REVEREND DR. MANTON EASTBURN,
BISHOP OF MASSACHUSETTS

WHEN as preacher at the consecration of Bishop Phillips Brooks I referred to the loneliness of a bishop's life, my remark awakened a strain of criticism which was curiously and pathetically denunciatory. Of course it came from people who knew nothing of what they were denouncing; and its acidity was the just measure of its ignorance. But those who indulged in such criticism, while they did not seek to understand a matter with which they were wholly unfamiliar, might easily, had they seen fit, have insisted upon a distinction between different kinds of loneliness, which ought always to be recognised. Any man whose functions are, in whatever measure, judicial, may wisely cultivate a good deal of reserve in their exercise. If, as has very often happened, he puts himself in

the hands of ecclesiastical counsellors who are
also ecclesiastical intimates, his judgments will
be suspected, and often deservedly, of having
a partisan note which greatly discounts their
value. And if, whatever his judgments, he
has only one set of intimates, two or three
of whom may easily be as able as, or abler
than, he, it will be strange if his official attitude towards those from whom he differs is
not sometimes partial and ungenerous. For
these reasons, therefore, the episcopate may
wisely bring with it the surrender of many in-
timacies ; and the denial of opportunities
which intellectual intimacy involves must
needs be, often, a costly and painful de-
privation.

But the moment that this is said, there is
something on the other side which needs to be
said, and of which the subject of this sketch
was a tragic illustration. It is possible to be
lonely from a sense of duty ; but, alas ! it is no
less possible to be isolated from choice ; and
this may come to pass almost, if not quite,
unconsciously.

Bishop Manton Eastburn was born in Leeds,
England, A.D. 1801, and came to the United
States when about twelve years old. He en-
tered Columbia College during his thirteenth

The Right Reverend
Doctor Manton Eastburn,
Bishop of Massachusetts.

From a photograph

The Right Reverend
Doctor Manton Eastburn,
Bishop of Massachusetts.
From a photograph.

year, and graduated at the age of sixteen. A
few years later he became a theological student, was ordained deacon and priest by Bishop
Hobart, and, after a brief service as an assistant minister in Christ Church, New York, became, in 1827, the first rector of the Church
of the Ascension, New York, where he ministered until, in 1842, he was elected Assistant
Bishop of Massachusetts. Bishop Griswold,
his senior, died within some six weeks of
Bishop Eastburn's consecration ; and, in 1843,
Bishop Eastburn was left in exclusive charge
of the Diocese of Massachusetts.

It illustrates the feebleness of the Church in
New England at that time that the Church
in Massachusetts could not support a bishop
who was not also a rector, and that Bishop
Eastburn had so little to do of an episcopal
nature that his visitations could all be completed during a few weeks' absence from his
parish in the spring and autumn. For the
rest of the year he could devote himself, unre-
servedly, as he did, to the ordinary duties of
the rectorship of Trinity Church.

That parish then enjoyed the advantage of
two endowments ; one for the maintenance of
a course of lectures instituted by means of what
was known as the Price Fund, and the other,

the Greene Foundation, a bequest by a parishioner of that name for the purpose of providing the parish with an assistant minister. The assistant minister had charge of the parish during the bishop's absence, and at other times preached once on Sunday, and divided with the bishop the other duties of the parish. To this office I was called about the time that I became secretary of the House of Bishops, and it brought me into a relationship with Bishop Eastburn which was equally interesting and unusual.

Unusual, I say, for I was so much the bishop's junior that, from the outset, his intercourse with me was alike affectionate and unreserved. The bishop was what might now be called an old-fashioned low-Churchman, and his preaching had that note of somewhat ponderous circumlocution from which, as I shall endeavour to show in speaking of Bishop Thomas M. Clark, some of his peers and contemporaries had already broken away. Bishop Phillips Brooks, who, as a lad, had sat under Bishop Eastburn's preaching, used to tell a story (I do not vouch for it) of having heard Bishop Eastburn, in a discourse on the rich man and Lazarus, refer to the prayer of the rich man, when in torment, that Lazarus might dip the tip of his finger in water and cool the rich man's tongue; and affirmed that the bishop, after quoting the verse in which these words occur, added, sententiously, " To this wholly inadmissible request the patriarch returned a negative reply."

But though this was characteristic of the bishop's style of pulpit utterance, his habit of conversation, as I remember it, was singularly informal and unreserved. Indeed, my own acquaintance with him began in a burst of candour on his part which, whether in directness or frankness, could not easily be matched. I had just been elected to the " Greene Foundation," and, at his own table, was dining with him for the first time. After dinner the bishop fidgeted in his chair, in a fashion that betrayed, plainly enough, his discomfort; and, springing at last from his seat, went to the sideboard and seized a box of cigars. Turning towards me as he did so, and remembering, I suppose, that I was the son of one who, as a college professor, had been widely known for his hostility to tobacco, he exclaimed, with a lugubrious expression which I can never forget, " Dr. Potter, I presume that you don't smoke ? "

" Whenever I can get a chance, I do," I

answered promptly. Whereupon, his whole face broadening into a smile of delighted surprise, he exclaimed, "Thank God! I was afraid that you had inherited the detestable prejudices of your father!"

Nothing could have been more entirely characteristic of Bishop Eastburn. Any man who differed from him, upon any conceivable subject, in theology or life, social, literary, or philosophical, was, from his point of view, the victim of a "detestable prejudice." He had made up the parcel of his opinions,—in what lights and under what influences I do not know,—had neatly tied them up with the red tape of a cherished tradition, and had deposited the package on the top shelf of his mental storehouse, not to be taken down or disturbed under any conceivable conditions. He was a scholar; and he had a sincere love of letters, which made him one of the best students of the classics whom I ever knew. Indeed, it was my commonest experience, whenever I entered his library, to find him with a volume of some Greek or Latin poet in his hand. But living, as he did, through an era which witnessed some of the most tremendous readjustments of Christian faith and dogma, he never, so far as I could learn, con-

sented to read a line of the authors who discussed them, or to talk about them or their
work with any one who had.

It was this mental attitude—it is not an un-
common one among theologians—that created
that pathetic isolation to which I have referred. It is unnecessary that I should remind my readers that Bishop Eastburn was
surrounded by an intellectual atmosphere, cultivated, acute, and supremely interrogative.
With one phase of this he was socially intimate ;
for, when I lived in Boston, he belonged to a
club whose meetings, on a week night, I have
always understood that he attended with considerable regularity, and where he met many
men, and discussed many subjects—or heard
them discussed—that must have taken his
mind far afield. But, so far as I could discover, no experience of this kind awakened in
him any curiosity, nor produced in him any
other mental process than to cling more closely
to his own opinions.

It was this mental characteristic, or habit,
that made his life an exceptionally lonely one,
and that grew upon him as years went on.
When I came to know him, he was a sep-
tuagenarian, and his points of view were
fixed and unchangeable. That, I suppose, is

characteristic of many men who are no longer young ; but in his case it had produced a frigidity of attitude, and an impatience of intellectual dissent, which left him pathetically isolated among the best minds of his generation. He loved a horse, and rode him well ; but no one, I apprehend, ever saw him pass along Beacon Street on horseback, on his way out of town, without being sensible of a certain note of loneliness in that solitary figure, which was profoundly touching.

For, underneath the somewhat chilly exterior, and the formal and reserved manner, there was a singularly warm and tender heart. The friends who loved him, loved him for qualities that were exceptionally noble and lovable. He was absolutely constant, and absolutely fearless ; and this last made of him a champion whose instinct of loyalty to a friend was at once chivalric and imperious. I was leaving his study one morning when the bell rang; and the bishop, stepping to a window that commanded the front door, said : " Wait a moment, Potter. Here comes a committee, and I should like to have you present while I receive them." The committee was from a suburban parish whose rector was a man already known by his pen, of eccentric habits, but of rare gifts. He had made himself obnoxious in the family of one of the vestry by declining to continue in it as a "table boarder" when he found the table impossible; and the committee had come, at the instigation of the lady whose table he had deserted, to denounce him as an opium-eater.

The bishop heard the charge (which I may say here was false) with a pained surprise, which he at once proceeded to express; and then, after a moment's pause, he said: "I suppose, gentlemen, you wish me to take canonical action in this painful business, and I shall proceed to do so. But, to that end, it is necessary that the charge should be presented to me in writing, and that you should subscribe your names to it." At this suggestion the faces of the committee underwent a sudden transformation, and with one accord they sprang to their feet, their spokesman exclaiming: "Oh, no, Bishop! We could n't do that! We don't want to sign anything. We merely wished to come and tell you what you have heard, and leave the matter in your hands. But we could n't sign any paper."

"No," said the bishop, while his whole form dilated with the indignation which was seething within him. "No! You will not stand behind

your charge, when you are called upon to do
it; but, though you know that a clergyman's
reputation is well-nigh as sensitive as a woman's,
you will do all that you can to destroy it; and
when you are asked to subscribe to your own
accusation you will refuse." The bishop had
risen from his seat, and was moving towards
his study door as he continued : " Do you know,
gentlemen, what the Rev. Dr. ——— would
do if he were a layman? *He would horsewhip
you*—and so would I! Good morning, gentlemen!" And the bishop swung open the door
and bowed them out.

One more scene recurs to me, which was
wholly different in the kindly temper that
inspired it, and yet was none the less memor-
able in that absolute candour which distinguished it. It was at the bishop's table, on
the evening of the consecration, as Bishop of
Central New York, of the late Dr. Frederic
Dan Huntington. On Bishop Eastburn's
right sat Bishop Clark of Rhode Island,
Bishop Coxe of Western New York, and
Bishop Randall of Colorado; and on his left
Bishop Horatio Potter of New York, Bishop
Littlejohn of Long Island, and Bishop Huntington of Central New York. As secretary
of the House of Bishops, I was at the foot of

the table, and was the only presbyter present.
When dinner was concluded, the bishop rose
in his place, and, holding a glass of wine in
his hand, said, after a few words of affectionate reference to the newly consecrated bishop,
" Brethren, I wish to propose his health ";
and then, after an instant's pause, "and I am
the only man at this table who has a right to
do it, for"— running his eye round the table
until it had included in its sweep every bishop
present—" I am the only born Churchman
among you ! "   I remember well the startled
pause that followed ; but he was right. Bishop
Clark had been born a Congregationalist ;
Bishop Coxe a Presbyterian ; Bishop Randall
a Baptist ; Bishop Horatio Potter a Quaker ;
Bishop Littlejohn a Presbyterian ; and Bishop
Huntington a Unitarian.   But no one among
them all, whatever the stern theological in-
tolerance of the host, had a larger heart or
a more enduring affection for his fellow-men.
When he had passed away, and when, in accordance with its rule, the House of Bishops
had concluded the simple office that recognised his departure, one of the least demonstra-
tive of his associates walked to the desk where
I was making a record of the bishop's death,
and putting his finger upon the name that I

had just written said, "I shall miss him greatly."
(They had not a theological conviction in common.) "He was the only man who always
called me 'Horatio'!"

Bishop Clark

V

𝔅𝔦𝔰𝔥𝔬𝔭 ℭ𝔩𝔞𝔯𝔨

THE RIGHT REVEREND DR. THOMAS MARCH
CLARK, BISHOP OF RHODE ISLAND

A VERY distinct and a very individual
figure in the House of Bishops for nearly
fifty years was that of the second Bishop of
Rhode Island, Dr. Thomas M. Clark, who was
in many respects less eminent as an ecclesiastic than as a teacher, a thinker, and a prophet.
He was of New England ancestry, and was
nurtured in the straitest sect of its Puritan
traditions and its Congregationalist theology.
He outgrew both of them, but he never forgot
them ; and the dominion which they exercised,
until the close of an unusually long life, over
his imagination, if not over his reason, was one
of the most pathetic facts in his history. While
a student at Princeton College, he came under
the influences that made of him a Churchman ;
and later, when a rector in Hartford, Conn., he
found himself a neighbour of one of the most

original and vigorous minds that this country has produced — I mean that of Dr. Horace Bushnell. In Dr. Bushnell's *Life* there are letters from Bishop Clark which disclose the influence of Dr. Bushnell, and the conditions under which it came to be exercised. Events move so rapidly, and changes during the last half century in the dogmatic positions of many Christian bodies have been so considerable, that it is not easy, to-day, to realise how absolute was the empire which certain theological traditions and usages exercised over the mind and speech of Bishop Clark until he had reached middle life. Of usage, I say, as well as of theological opinions; for in one particular Bishop Clark was the leader, at any rate in his own Communion, of a departure from what was counted as the rhetorical usage of the pulpit, as noteworthy as it was radical. When the Rev. Thomas M. Clark began his ministry the usage in preaching was to be stately, ponderous, and somewhat circumlocutory. The last thing that a preacher dreamed of doing was to call a spade a spade; and when Bishop Clark broke with the accustomed usage it was the introduction of a startling novelty. As a lad, I was wont to follow him about with a dog-like devotion when he came to Philadelphia, where

The Right Reverend
Doctor Thomas March Clark,
Bishop of Rhode Island.
From a photograph by Naegeli, New York.

in his earlier ministry he had been settled.
He was once preaching in St. Stephen's
Church, Philadelphia, from the story of Naaman's cleansing and conversion, as given in
2 Kings v., and his text was : " In this thing
the Lord pardon thy servant, that when my
master goeth into the house of Rimmon to
worship there, and he leaneth on my hand,
and I bow myself in the house of Rimmon ;
when I bow down myself in the house of Rimmon, the Lord pardon thy servant in this
thing." (V. 18.) In other words, Naaman had
been cleansed of his leprosy by Elisha, and had
professed his faith in the God of Israel. But
he was a servant of the King of Syria, and his
master was a pagan. He would be obliged,
when in attendance upon the king, to go into
a pagan temple, and he asked, in advance, to
be forgiven if, outwardly, he conformed to its
usages.

As was not unnatural, the preacher used the
incident to illustrate the unworthiness of a half-
hearted service ; and waxing warm he said—in
that pathetic tenor voice of his which no one
who ever heard it will forget—" I am not unmindful, my dear brethren, that Naaman asked
of the prophet two mules' burden of earth
wherewith to erect an altar to the true God : but

I have no doubt, that if we could have followed him to that far-off land to which he returned, we should have found that he carted the earth into the back yard and dumped it there, and that that was the end of it."

I was but a small boy that afternoon, but I can remember as though it had happened yesterday the shock which this familiar imagery gave to that polished congregation. The "back yard," and the " dumping" were figures unfamiliar to pulpit rhetoric as they knew it, but they "sat up," understanding it, and did not go to sleep !

No one did who listened to Bishop Clark. In the House of Bishops he was not a frequent speaker, but when he rose to his feet, his brethren paused from whatever tasks that were engaging them, and gave to him their undivided attention. He saw large questions in a large light ; and upon a discussion which was running in somewhat narrow and conventional ruts he would sometimes descend with a few pungent and illuminative sentences which cleared the whole air.

Added to this was a sense of humour which, coupled with his intimate knowledge of Scripture, was simply irresistible. The incident which I am about to relate has often been imputed to one who preceded him in the office of Presiding Bishop, but inaccurately. A Presiding Bishop, senior to both of them, and whose Christian name was Benjamin, was attempting, on one occasion, to explain his action in a matter of ecclesiastical discipline, which had been widely criticised. As he proceeded, it became plain that his explanation was likely only to involve the whole subject in deeper mystery; and as the bishop went on, piling one obscure or contradictory statement on top of another, until the whole subject became hopelessly involved, and unintelligible, Bishop Clark passed my desk, and by a dexterous backward movement of his hand projected a small roll of paper across the page on which I was writing. Unrolling it unsuspectingly I read, "But Benjamin's *mess* was five times so much as any of theirs."[1] The situation could not have been more accurately described!

But it would be a very inaccurate impression of Bishop Clark to suppose that levity or frivolity was the dominant note of his character. The old proverb which describes the fountains of laughter and tears lying very close together never had a more striking

[1] Gen. xliii., 34.

illustration than in the mind of Bishop Clark. On the one hand, there was his Puritan ancestry, with its theology of gloom and despair,—its familiar axiom being that one was not fit to be saved until he was willing to be damned ; and with him there was a keen sense of the comic, a delightful sensitiveness to the incongruous, which made of his companionship an unceasing entertainment.   One morning when I was a New York rector he came into my study, saying, "I am going abroad for six months."   As my relations with the bishop were more than usually confidential, and I knew how many demands were made upon his purse, I was somewhat puzzled to imagine how the pecuniary problem, in this somewhat costly undertaking, was to be solved ; and I said bluntly, " How are you going to manage it?"

" This is the way that I am going to manage it," answered the bishop, throwing down on the table a cheque for twenty-five hundred dollars.   The cheque was drawn by the late Mr. Robert Bonner, proprietor, at that time, of the New York *Ledger*.

" What is this for?" I asked, and the bishop answered :

" For twenty-five articles for the *Ledger*."

" Have you written them?" I asked.

" Oh, no," replied the bishop, " but I shall—
some of them—while on shipboard."

" And what will they be about?" I per-
sisted in enquiring, wondering at the fertility
which could so surely count upon itself.

" On the moral uses of hairpins, and subjects of that character," said the bishop, without
the ripple of a smile upon his grave features.

And, if one had followed the workings of
that curiously speculative mind, he would have
been amazed to find from how many sources,
quite as humble and insignificant, some of his
gravest reflections sprang!

His mind had in one word that rare charm
which Martineau somewhere depicts in a discourse in which he distinguishes between child-
ishness and childlikeness. Bishop Clark never
could be childish, but, in that almost weird
sense of wonder which all things in heaven
and in earth seemed to awaken in him, he
could touch and transform the lowliest things
of life and make them pregnant with meaning
to every age. His genius was never ade-
quately recognised, but it will never be forgotten by those who felt its spell.

Bishop Core

VI

𝔅𝔦𝔰𝔥𝔬𝔭 𝔠𝔬𝔵𝔢

THE RIGHT REVEREND DR. ARTHUR CLEVELAND
COXE, BISHOP OF WESTERN NEW YORK

THERE lies before me a volume of Church
History, in which is a sketch of Bishop
Coxe, and others of his brethren ; and the
preface makes a high claim for its painstaking
statistical accuracy. I have not the smallest
doubt that that claim is abundantly warranted
by the exactness and precision with which
every date has been cited, and every product
of the pen of an exceptionally prolific author
set down. But to call that history, is much as
though one should place on the table before
us a jar containing the ashes of a dead friend,
and then say, " Here is the man whom you
have loved and lost." One would be something more or less than human if he did not
reply, " All honour to these sacred *manes* ! I
cannot look at yonder vase without deep
and keen emotion. But the friend whom I

have lost—he is not there !   That is not he !"

And something like that must needs be the
instinctive cry of any one who reads any recollections of Bishop Coxe.   No matter how
vivid they may be, he was somehow more
vital, more vivid, more engaging !   No matter
how familiarly his life moved along wonted
ecclesiastical lines, the man who moved within
them was anything but familiar or commonplace.   He had a keen sense of decorum, and
he never forgot to bear himself as became his
breeding and his calling.   But neither of these
could extinguish in him that rare light which
marked him off from other men, and which
was the light of genius !   I have been told that
there were "plain people" who thought him
fanciful, hyper-sensitive, "notional."   So much
the worse, then, one would be constrained to
say, for the "plain people" !   A lark's note,
waking one out of a stupid and heavy sleep,
has been regarded as an impertinent intru-
sion ; and I have seen very worthy but very
dull men in the House of Bishops regarding
Bishop Coxe, when he burst into some fine
frenzy, almost as they would have stared at
an escaped lunatic.   But one could only regret
the opacity of their vision, and mourn the absence, in them, of the gift of imagination.

The Right Reverend
Doctor Arthur Cleveland Coxe,
Bishop of Western New York.
From a photograph by Naegeli, New York.

The Right Reverend
Doctor Arthur Cleveland Coxe,
Bishop of Western New York.

From a photograph by Naegeli, New York.

My own acquaintance with Bishop Coxe began when he was rector of Grace Church,
Baltimore, in the vestry of which was a gentleman who was a friend of my parents, and in
whose house, when I was an undergraduate in
the Theological Seminary of Virginia, I was
often a guest. The Rev. Dr. Coxe was an intimate and honoured friend of the family, and
I then came under the spell of a personality
which had a singular charm and attractiveness.
At that time the courtlier manners of our
fathers still survived, and were still to be encountered, at any rate, among the clergy. They
had not been conspicuous among my theological preceptors, though these were men of rare
benignity and of noble temper : and I confess
that, to a young student who emerged, now
and then, from a somewhat austere and un-
ceremonious atmosphere, there was something
singularly engaging in these occasional visits
to Baltimore, with its fine mixture of Southern
warmth and stately breeding ; and in the delightful bearing of one who, Northerner though
he was, had caught its best traits, and was
persona simpatica (as our Italian friends say)
with its best social ideals.

But nothing would be more unjust than to
infer from this that Dr. Coxe was simply a

" society " parson ; and still more unjust would
be the conclusion that he had any penchant for
that somewhat convivial note which, when I
first knew it, was a recognisable characteristic
of a charming city. A friend, himself a parson, who, as a great host of friends did, enjoyed the freedom of the ever-hospitable house
to which I have referred, told me this story,
which is both illustrative of a layman's conception of an appropriate expression of his
devotion to his pastor, and of Dr. Coxe's indifference in any convivial direction. The divine to whom I have referred arrived at his
friend's house during the host's absence, and
was served, through the kind assiduity of the
hostess, with the best in the house that she
could lay her hands on. After a day or two
her husband returned, and she said to him,
" Mr. W——, I think that was very poor
claret that you left out for Dr. J——."

" It was," answered her husband, " but he did
not know it. I have had one lesson which has
taught me never to waste anything good on
the clergy. You know how I loved Dr. Coxe :
well, when he left Baltimore I gave him six
bottles of that X Madeira. You know its
value. It was *priceless*. It was worth its
weight in gold ; and if I had had a bottle

of that Madeira at my right hand and its weight in gold on the left I would have taken the Madeira! As you will remember, I was in New York last winter, and went, one day, to Dr. Coxe's church. He saw me, and sent the sexton to ask me, after service, to come into the rectory to lunch. I did so, and, at table, the rector pressed upon me all that it offered, until at length I said, 'Thank you, I am not very well—indeed I am rather faint; and I wonder, Doctor, if I could have a glass of that Madeira that I gave you, when you left Baltimore?'

"'Certainly,' said the rector, turning to the lady who presided at the other end of the table; 'Lucy, dear, where is that Madeira that Mr. W—— gave us?'

"'Why, don't you remember, my love?' said the lady of the house; 'I used it to wash the baby with!'

"Now then," added Mr. W—— to his wife, "do you think that, after that, I am going to trouble myself to set out anything choice for a parson?"

And most hosts, I presume, would have agreed with him,—especially if the subject of these recollections had been the guest, for no one could have been more profoundly indifferent to the pleasures of the table than he.

For decorum, however, he had a most scrupulous regard; and one or two instances of this recur to me which were pre-eminently characteristic. The General Convention of 1871 sat in Baltimore, and its most distinguished guest was Bishop Selwyn, then Bishop of Lichfield; but first of all, Bishop of New Zealand, where he had illustrated a heroism of the noblest quality. Bishop Coxe, whose admiration for everything Anglican was a very conspicuous trait, was most anxious that everything about the convention should be as stately and refined as the surroundings in the mother country to which the distinguished guest was wonted; and to that end visited, a few hours before the convention opened, the hall in which the bishops were to sit. In its vestibule, to his horror, he found, stacked up, two or three dozens of "stone China" spittoons; and, rushing into the hall, he called out:

"Dr. Potter, have you seen this pyramid of horrors in the vestibule? Surely, you are not going to allow them to be brought into the House of Bishops? Think what an impression they will produce upon our English guest!"

"Alas, my dear Bishop," I answered, "I

have no discretion in the matter. If I do
not provide them to-day, I shall be ordered to
do so to-morrow. The Bishops of A. and B.
and C., and others, will refuse to be deprived
of a convenience to which they and many
others have long been accustomed."

" A convenience ! " cried the bishop.   " Is it
possible that we are such a tribe of savages ! "
and, banging the door behind him, he vanished
in a fine rage.

Of course, there was a comic side to all this ;
but it was none the less the chivalrous sensi-
bility of a finely strung nature, often unintelligible to men of coarser mould ; and I am afraid
that we jested about it, sometimes, after a
fashion that was not creditable.   One *escapade*
of this nature I can now recall in which I was
the chief offender, and by making frank con-
fession of it, here, I may perhaps, in part at
least, atone for an act of which I was long ago
ashamed.

During a General Convention which sat in
New York while I was secretary of the House
of Bishops, a man of letters, at that time one
of the editors of a leading periodical still widely
read, asked a number of bishops to dine with
him at the Union Club, and the peals of laughter which distinguished the feast found their

way down-stairs to the ears of the clubmen below. One of these, a member of the family with which Bishop Coxe was staying, gave the bishop an account of the occasion, which the bishop brought with him to the meeting of the House next morning. He repeated it to me in terms which seemed to me exaggerated and luridly denunciatory. " The thing was a grave breach of ecclesiastical propriety, and the bishops who had been guilty of it should be brought to the bar of the House and publicly reprimanded."

The whole story struck me, I confess, as grotesque and extravagant, and presented an opportunity for ridicule which, to the presumption of youth, was too tempting to be resisted. After the bishop, therefore, had finished his recital, and had gone to his seat, or rather to two or three adjacent bishops, to whom he had repeated the story, I drew up a mock *indictment*, garnishing it with certain phrases of the bishop's, easily recognisable, and passed it across to a bishop sitting near me. After extracting from it the mirth which it afforded him, he handed it to his neighbour ; and, seeing that it was likely to "go the rounds," I turned to the task before me. Imagine, if you can, my horror and amazement, when, a little

later, feeling a hand upon my shoulder, I looked
up and saw Bishop Coxe with an expression of
wrath upon his face which froze me with terror;
and my unfortunate paper in his other hand!

"Dr. Potter," he whispered, "this has just
been handed to me by one of my brethren"
(I never have been able to discover who this
episcopal meddler was) "and it was written, I
suppose,—this travesty of my just indignation,
—by some bishop in this House. I shall bring
it to the notice of the House, and demand that
its author declare himself!" I looked at the
bishop, and then at the paper—in which I may
say that I had not made the slightest effort to
disguise my handwriting,—and caught desper-
ately at the one loop-hole of escape. "Do
you think, Bishop," I said, "that such a thing
as that is worthy of your notice? Do you
care to betray to the House of Bishops that
you can be hurt by such a production as that?
Do nothing about it, now, and leave the whole
matter until after recess, when, I am persuaded,
you will feel that that paper deserves only
your contempt. Meanwhile, leave it with me."
The bishop left me, and returned, with troubled
countenance, to his seat. So soon as the hour
of recess came, I took the wretched paper into
the back-yard and burnt it. Do you think you

would like to have been in my place when,
after recess, I saw the bishop rise from his seat
and approach mine?   He placed his hand on
my shoulder, and bent over me to demand, as
I tremblingly anticipated, the return of the
paper. But no. Instead, he said, " Dr. Potter,
you are a wise man. That paper *was* unworthy
of my notice.   Destroy it, if you will.   I shall
concern myself no further about it."   And the
incident was happily concluded.

But I shall regret having recalled it if any
who may read it, now, shall fail to see in it,
comic as were some of its aspects, that fine
sense of fitness which lent to all that Bishop
Coxe was and did, a supreme charm.   Like
another of whom the Scriptures speak, he was
" very jealous" for all that concerned the
honour of his high calling ; and through all
that he said and was, there shone the lustre of a
courage as heroic as it was unfamiliar. Ridicule,
vituperation, clamour—they could not turn
him aside ; and when the Church lost him it
lost not alone its foremost poet, a rare scholar,
an untiring prelate, a pre-eminently picturesque figure upon the canvas of its chequered
history, but, most of all, a moral hero !

Bishop Wilmer

VII

Bishop Wilmer

THE RIGHT REVEREND DR. JOSEPH PERE BELL
WILMER, BISHOP OF LOUISIANA

DURING the General Convention of 1895, which sat in the city of Minneapolis, Minn., I remember very well being arrested in some task in which at the moment I was engaged, by two figures that, in eager conversation, were withdrawing from the House of Bishops — the Bishop of Western New York, the Right Reverend Arthur Cleveland Coxe, and the Bishop of Minnesota, the Right Reverend Henry Benjamin Whipple. Standing near me, at the moment, was a junior bishop who had but just taken his seat in the House for the first time, and to whom most of its members were unknown.

" Look at those two men," I said, " for they represent our most picturesque element. There are other bishops in this House as learned, as devout, as self-sacrificing, as they.

95

But none of them is *picturesque*. Bishops
Coxe and Whipple are picturesque."

If my right reverend junior had entered
the House of Bishops a few years earlier, he
would have found there a bishop who died in
1878, and who, in some respects more picturesque than either of those whom I have
named, was indeed one of the most interesting
and charming illustrations that the House has
known of qualities that were neither mechani-
cal, nor commonplace.

Joseph Pere Bell Wilmer was born early in
the nineteenth century, in New Jersey; but
his ancestry was Southern, and he early found
his way to Virginia, where he was a student
both at the University of Virginia and the
Alexandria Seminary. Here, in 1834, he was
ordained deacon by Bishop Richard Chan-
ning Moore, and later, by the same prelate, a
priest. His earliest rectorship was at Albe-
marle, Virginia, from which he went, later, to
the University of the State as chaplain, and
later (in 1839) into the United States Navy.
Four years later he resigned his office as Navy
chaplain, and became a rector in Virginia.
When I first knew him I was a child, and he
was rector of St. Mark's Church, Philadelphia,
in my father's diocese.

The Right Reverend
Doctor Joseph Pere Bell Wilmer,
Bishop of Louisiana.
From a photograph by Washburn, New Orleans.

The Right Reverend
Doctor Joseph Pere Bell Wilmer,
Bishop of Louisiana.
From a photograph by Washburn, New Orleans.

Already, then, I became sensible, mere lad though I was, of a certain "aloofness" in him, which made one conscious that he was a person wont to commune with high thoughts and themes, and not easily descending to commonplace men and thoughts. I shall have gravely misrepresented him, if it is inferred from this that he was cold, or supercilious, or in any way distant. Nothing could be farther from the fact. The first impression which one derived from him was of his singular gentleness, tenderness, and benignity. He could not be frigid or reserved; but one was often sensible that, when his attention was summoned to ordinary things, he was like one who "came down from the mount."

And mixed with all this was a touch of matchless humour, which was all the more potential because so absolutely unconscious. On one occasion, when the House of Bishops was sitting in special session in Philadelphia for the purpose of filling two or three vacancies in the missionary episcopate, that body was treated to a series of nominations of very young and wholly unknown men, by bishops who, because their nominees were so little known to the House, were tempted to describe them and their gifts in somewhat extravagant language.

After the nominations were concluded, the House, in accordance with its custom, adjourned. An opportunity was thus afforded for private enquiry; and the election occurred next morning. Just before we were about to proceed to it, Bishop Wilmer rose in his place, and, with a manner of awe-inspiring solemnity, began:

"Mr. President, yesterday afternoon in undertaking to return to this House, I lost my way. [No one was surprised at this, knowing the abstracted and unobservant habits of the bishop.] In seeking to recover it [he went on], I wandered into a graveyard, and found myself reading the inscriptions upon the tombstones. It was evidently the place where the *good* Philadelphians are buried; and such an assemblage of the great and virtuous, I said to myself, I had never encountered. But, as I said so, I remembered the panegyrics to which I had listened, yesterday morning, in this House;—remembered them, and realised that it is not always necessary for ordinary and commonplace people to be dead in order to be over-praised!"

And then, as if the graver aspect of the subject had suddenly broken upon him, the bishop added, with a fine burst of passion:

"Sir, I am tired of these extravagant eulogies upon these unknown and insignificant boys! The Church has no use, either in the missionary field or anywhere else, for these Tulchan-bishops,—these calf bishops, as they would be, if elected; and, for myself, sir [said the bishop, sweeping the House with an eye that flashed fire, and pausing as his look caught the upturned face of Bishop Arthur Cleveland Coxe, of Western New York], for myself, sir, if the Church needs more missionary bishops I want such bishops as my brother, yonder—the Bishop of *Buffalo*, as he ought to be called, as he goes up and down his diocese tossing his horns at Puritan and Papist alike ! "

The bishop took his seat, and the young nominees were not elected. But, before we adjourned, the elegant and gracious Bishop of Western New York, whose only claim to be called the " Bishop of Buffalo " consisted in the fact that he lived in that city, came to the secretary's table, and, putting his hand on my shoulder, whispered, " Dr. Potter, *do* I look like a buffalo ? "

The vagrant instincts of Bishop Wilmer did not always content themselves with obstructive activities. I recall an incident which occurred just after our Civil War, and which was strikingly illustrative of qualities in the bishop as rare as they were noble. Bishop Wilmer was chosen to succeed the lamented Polk, just at the conclusion of the Civil War ; and the General Convention which met in New York in October, 1868, was the first at which he was present after his consecration, two years earlier.

It was not, in many respects, a congenial assemblage to the bishop. The tragic events of the Civil War were too recent, the South, in her broken and impoverished condition, was made, in too many ways, painfully conscious of the poverty and feebleness of the Church in the South, as her bishops, clergy, and laity gathered in brilliant New York; and Bishop Wilmer was pre-eminently a Southerner. As a consequence, the House of Bishops saw very little of him. He would appear in his place in the morning; answer to his name, when it was called; assist in the devotions of the day; and then, after lingering a little, with a face pathetic in its sadness, and pre-eminently expressive in its utter absence of any token of interest in the business of the hour, quietly steal away. The rest of the morning and the afternoon were spent in wandering about the streets with an air which those who met him described as indicating infinite weariness and *ennui*. But his mind was not vacant, nor his purpose without aim. On one such occasion, a passerby observed him standing in front of a great commercial house, and staring up at its stately proportions with an air which might, not unnaturally, have been described as one of vacant curiosity. After a few moments' hesitation, he entered the building, asked for the proprietor, and sent in his name. As it happened, the great merchant was disengaged, received the bishop courteously, and, albeit with some amusement at first, listened to him patiently. For the bishop, as those who knew him will remember was not infrequently his custom, began to generalise. Here about him he saw, he said, the evidences of a vast business, and was warranted, he presumed, in inferring from it large returns and great wealth. But wealth, like any other human power, or possession, implied stewardship; and large stewardship involved large peril. The interview ended with a personal application of the whole argument, of infinite tenderness and directness. The merchant, who, it may be said, by the way, was not an irreligious man, but a church-goer, and then, at any rate, a man of exemplary walk and conversation, said, later, in recounting this incident, "In all my life, no one ever spoke to me like that!" The issue of this interview, an issue that most vividly expressed, to many minds, the profound impression which it made, was a gift of princely munificence to a diocese contiguous to New York for the erection and endowment of a cathedral.

The informality which distinguished his action in seeking this merchant, and speaking to him as he did, was pre-eminently characteristic of Bishop Wilmer. He had a sublime indifference to mere conventionalisms, and that it was not customary to break in upon a man of business in order to press upon his attention great spiritual considerations did not influence him in the smallest degree. It was the same trait of which I had an eminently characteristic illustration a few years later. I happened to be in New Orleans during the session of the Diocesan Convention; and, after dining with the bishop, was asked to accompany him to an evening session of the convention. It was a wild night when we set out, with the rain descending in torrents; and as we neared the church in which the convention was to assemble, we were obliged to cross the street. I do not know how it may be now, but, in those days, the drainage of New Orleans was surface-drainage—at any rate so far as the rainfall was concerned; and, in order to meet those very frequent emergencies when the wide and deep gutters on each side of the street were swollen with water, stepping-stones were provided, by means of which one could cross the street. We started to do this, but alas, the bishop was absorbed in an animated narration, and turning, for the moment, missed his footing, and, literally, disappeared in the flood. So soon as was possible, I seized him and dragged him out, drenched and dripping, of course, and without a dry stitch upon him.

"You must go home, sir, and change your clothes!" I exclaimed, so soon as I could command breath to speak.

"Not at all," answered the bishop. "It is too late for that; and, moreover, I read my annual address this evening. I must borrow from the neighbourhood what I need."

It was a long way back to the bishop's house; and if it had not been, it was plain that the bishop was determined not to return thither. So we hurried on to the vestry room of the church, where the bishop removed his dripping garments, and put on such as his courteous lay neighbours provided.

Their colour and shape were not material, for, over all, the bishop was to wear his robes; but their size involved a very serious problem, for the average Southerner was "slim" and slender of figure, while the bishop's girth was portly and—considerable. However, by some simple ingenuity, we overcame this difficulty; and as I had known the bishop since I was a boy, he was amiable enough to allow me to secure his trousers and other nether-garments by a contrivance of loops of string which girthed him sufficiently for any ordinary emergency.

Yes ; but not for an extraordinary emergency ! The bishop delivered his address from a platform ; and as questions of ritual were, at the moment, much in the air, he discussed them with an impassioned oratory which all who knew him will remember. I had followed him into the church, and had taken my seat in a pew, not unnaturally somewhat elated at the success of my sartorial ingenuity. But my elation was of brief duration. With every moment the bishop became more impassioned ; his action more vehement ; the movements of his swaying and vibrating figure more pronounced and saltatory, until I found myself watching him in a cold perspiration, and anticipating with horror the dreaded moment *when a string should break !* Fortunately, it did n't.

It has been my good fortune, in searching for information in regard to Bishop Wilmer's earlier life, to find, in the recollections of his son, William N. Wilmer, Esq., a layman of New York of rare gifts and engaging character, most valued help, for which I desire here to make grateful acknowl-

edgment.   Says Mr. Wilmer, speaking of
his father :

"While no lengthy sketch of the Right Rev. J. P.
B. Wilmer, sometime Bishop of Louisiana, was ever
written, yet some of the characteristics of his life have
been perpetuated by certain experiences that have been
recalled by his contemporaries and others with whom he
was associated during his long and varied career. Some
of these incidents or anecdotes illustrate not only his
deep faith and devotion to the cause of religion, but also
illustrate his broadness and practical methods in dealing
with humanity.

" There was nothing unusual in Bishop Wilmer's boyhood, which was largely spent on the Eastern shore of
Maryland. As a boy he went for a time to school in
Philadelphia, and as the relatives with whom he was
staying attended rather a fashionable church, young
Wilmer acquired a great distaste for church and religion; but later on, when he was again at Philadelphia attending school, he was with people who went to a very
humble church where the congregation was composed
largely of poor people. It was at this time that religion
appeared to him in a different light, and he first began
to look upon it from a different standpoint. While his distaste and distrust of religion was first changed under the
influence of this humble little church, and the example
of this poor but earnest congregation, yet he did not
finally decide to go into the ministry until several years
thereafter. And it was the recollection of this little,
humble parish and congregation, and the reality of
religion that was there presented, which developed in
him a desire to be a minister.

" As illustrating his boyish character, it is told of him that on one occasion he had at college, a difference with a young man, whose conduct young Wilmer thought was so reprehensible that he should either apologise or be punished; consequently, as the fairest means of adjusting such differences, it was agreed that young Wilmer and his opponent should meet and settle the matter in the usual way that boys adopt. The day before the meeting, the young man came to Wilmer, and announced that, as he had to go away, a friend would take his place in settling their differences. Thereupon Wilmer replied that it was not a matter that required any delay, and that such suggestion of a substitute was an evidence of cowardice, as well as of impudence. He took the young man by the neck, and very quickly it was apparent that no delay or substitute was necessary, and the young man quickly repented of his wrong-doing. It is needless to say that Wilmer's attitude was approved by his fellow-students. With the same promptness that he had punished this young man he likewise made up with him, and was ever ready to aid him in case of need. These incidents are merely recalled to show the early qualities of the character of this earnest man, and to show that in early life he had the same weaknesses and shortcomings as other boys.

" Bishop Wilmer's early ministry began as a missionary in the mountains of Virginia; then he was a chaplain in the Navy; afterwards he had a church on the Eastern shore of Virginia; later he was rector of St. Mark's Church, Philadelphia; and his life closed as Bishop of Louisiana. While Bishop Wilmer was of a nervous, active temperament, yet in hours of danger he showed unusual calmness and self-control. It is told of him by one of his old associates who was with him on a voyage, that, in the midst of a great storm, when the ship was being tossed about by a heavy sea and the passengers were consequently in a state of great excitement (for it was generally considered that the situation was very dangerous), the bishop took up a very prominent position on the deck and began reading a newspaper. The effect on the passengers was quite magical, and so quickly diverted attention and produced such a change of feeling, that, when all danger was passed, the captain came forward and thanked him for his wonderful self-control and self-forgetfulness, and their consequent effect on the other people. It is stated that Mr. Wilmer, with a smile on his face, and in his rather inimitable way, turned to the captain and said: 'It was well, Captain, that my fellow-passengers did not examine the situation too closely; for they might have discovered that my newspaper was turned upside down;—therefore I deserve no credit for what was only feigned courage.'

" This incident is merely referred to as illustrating the readiness of the bishop to rise to emergencies, and to be helpful on all occasions, and yet modestly to disdain credit, as his subsequent career disclosed. In his very watchful care and guidance of his sons he always tried to impress upon them the importance of self-forgetfulness, and to spur them on to attempt what might be considered, even by others, impossible. When one of his boys had gone through a very severe ordeal and struggle he wrote him as follows:

'Whatever I have done in life to aid my fellows has usually been the result of overcoming the severest obstacles; and I would urge you, my dear boy, to struggle, and never to turn back or away from what is said to be impossible. In fact, "the impossible" is what may often most need your strength, your self-forgetfulness, and your courage.'

"The bishop was a man who was ever ready to give his sympathy to those in need, and was always on the alert to help the helpless or defend the defenceless. It is told of him that, on one occasion when he was travelling on the railroad, he noticed the conductor treating a poor, humble woman rather rudely; whereupon the bishop interceded, and in a kind and friendly way endeavoured to see if he could not do something to help both the woman and the conductor. But the conductor replied in a somewhat abusive tone; and thereupon the bishop, taking in the situation at a glance, stated with considerable firmness that he intended to protect the woman and that, in due time, the conductor would have to look for some other occupation. He then gave the conductor his address so that he might understand from whom to expect a complaint. Within twelve hours the conductor was removed from his position, and came to the bishop for aid, and as might be expected, the bishop, feeling the man had received a lesson, worked with the same earnest determination to have this reformed conductor reinstated, as he had worked to protect the poor woman. The conductor was reinstated, a better and a wiser man.

"In great emergencies the bishop was always on the alert, and rose to the occasion; and his courage, his sympathy, and sense of humour all combined to enable him to take advantage of any opportunity that needed these qualities, separately, or collectively. On one occasion, during the great railway strike in Pennsylvania, when he was called North, on a hurried trip, the train

upon which he was came suddenly to a stop near Pittsburg, and it was soon apparent that the strikers, and the
sympathisers with the strikers, had all gathered around
the train, where they were everywhere in evidence, and refused to allow the train to proceed or return. The bishop
was in the rear coach, and soon saw the situation. He
went to the rear platform, and after removing his hat, remained silent for a few moments; raised his voice in
strong tones, so as to attract attention, and asked the
crowd if they would allow him to tell them a story.
While the bishop was not a tall man, yet he had rather a
commanding presence, and his personality and presence
was the more striking and forcible whenever he was in
the midst of danger, for there was a firmness and fearlessness in manner as well as in voice, that invited immediate attention. After quiet was somewhat restored,
the bishop said: 'I have just come from a country
where we had some trouble not long ago [meaning the
South, and referring to the War], and it was a kind
of trouble that we do not want again, for we were
whipped, and many of you must have done the whip-
ping. So you can understand that I am rather afraid of
troubles of this sort, but my position here to-day reminds me of a story which I have lately heard, and
which may enable you to sympathise with me. As you
know, we have a great many coloured people down in
my country; and they are beginning to be educated,
and, consequently, they like to use great, big words,
whether such words have any meaning or not. Some
time ago I heard of a coloured preacher, who was scolding his congregation in language which neither he nor
they exactly understood, but he closed by saying that in
life there were only two roads to take, and he exhorted
his hearers to make their selection then and there.

" One road," he said, " leads to perdition, and the other
road leads to damnation." Whereupon an old coloured
brother in the far end of the church rose up and called
out: " If dem is the roads, den I 'll take to the woods."
'Now,' said the bishop, 'this is just my position. I understand that these are the only roads that I now have
before me, for the reason that you are unwilling that we
should go *up* the track, or *down* the track, so I do not
know what to do. It is needless to say that I would be
very grateful to you if you would n't force me and my
friends to take to the woods.' With a smile, but with a
somewhat earnest expression, the bishop replaced his hat
and bowed to the crowd, which sent up a deafening cheer
and soon the order was issued that ' the bishop's train '
should proceed, and it did proceed, and it was the only
train that passed over the road for several days.

" While the bishop was a man of great firmness, and
ready to face danger in any form, yet he was as simple
as a child, and his very simplicity and his faith in
human nature, as well as in the Great Creator, often
enabled him to do things which seemed impossible to
others. Like many men of his type, he was very forget-
ful and absent-minded, and very frequently lost papers.
On one occasion, when he went to England to attend the
Pan-Anglican Conference, he found he had left his letter
of credit at home. The other bishops with him asked him
what he was going to do about it. He said: ' I 'll just go
to the bankers, and ask them to give me another.' The
bishops laughed at the idea, and declared that it would be
impossible for him to get such a favor from them. Several
of them went with him to the bank, and remained in the
waiting-room, curious to see the result. Before long
the bishop came out. ' Well ? ' questioned the bishops.
' They gave me the letter,' he said, ' and have tele-

graphed the banker in the United States.' 'Well, we
are surprised,' they said, ' but you look so like a bishop
that they could not refuse you.'

" It was not that he looked so much like a bishop, but
that he had such an earnest, trustful expression, as well
as magnetic presence, that it seemed impossible for any
one to refuse any appeal that he should make. He
trusted others, and others could not refuse the temptation to trust him. He received back what he gave forth.
His innocency of life, and purity of thought, made him
a most sympathetic and helpful companion of those in
trouble; and his self-forgetfulness, and his vigorous
courage, made him an irresistible antagonist of the wrong-
doer. While he was deeply absorbed with the spiritual
life and religious growth of Louisiana, yet he did not
flinch from any responsibility in any practical matters
that seemed to be for the best interest of the State, or
the people at large. During the Reconstruction period
in Louisiana, when there was great danger of bloodshed,
at a time when Carpet-bag government was in existence,
it seemed necessary that some one not identified with the
political or partisan interests in the State should come
forward and present the matter to General Grant and
President-elect Hayes. At this juncture, some of the
Judges of the Supreme Court of Louisiana and other
prominent persons appealed to Bishop Wilmer to go to
Washington and see President Grant. While many people urged the bishop not to participate in what seemed
to be a strictly secular or worldly work, yet he did not
hesitate, as soon as he realised that it might be a call to
duty; so he promptly went to Washington and saw General Grant, and then to Columbus, Ohio, and saw President-elect Hayes; and the private letters which Bishop

Wilmer received, some of them addressed to President-elect Hayes and others written by him, clearly indicate that his mission was successful, and convinced the authorities as to what should be their duty; consequently the threatened period of bloodshed was averted, and the bishop returned to Louisiana as the bearer of the messages of peace and good will.

" In his religious life, while the bishop was strictly loyal to his particular creed, yet he was broad and sympathetic with all denominations and classes. He felt the importance of individual and church discipline and order, but he recognised and respected the views of others.

" His mission in life seemed to be to uplift the standard of manhood, and at the same time encourage peace and good will among all men. On one occasion, when he was visiting one of the country parishes in his diocese, he heard that there was danger of a serious trouble in a small Roman Catholic church, arising between the pastor and the congregation. He immediately sought the first opportunity of going to the church and appearing before the congregation. Not wishing to violate any of the rules of the church, he did not go into the chancel, but stood in the body of the church and made an appeal to the congregation on behalf of their religious duty, irrespective of individual feelings. He said in substance as follows: 'Owing to the absence of your own bishop and the difficulty of his getting to you within a reasonable time, I have taken the liberty to come before you and appeal to you, not as members of any particular sect, but as a body of religious people who owe a duty to themselves, to their bishop, and to their pastor. I am not here to defend your pastor or to defend you. The difficulties between you and him are not for me to consider; but I do appeal to you, as a body of people who gather here in this sacred building for a sacred purpose, to try to restrain your feelings, and control your impulses, and subdue your prejudices. Let me earnestly request of you, in the name of your absent bishop, if I may be permitted to do so, and urge upon you all, pastor and congregation, a united effort to suspend judgment upon each other, and to try and live harmoniously together, if not permanently, at least until your bishop can come to you and hear and know your troubles.' It is needless to say that the trouble subsided between the people and pastor, and that the Bishop of Louisiana evidenced in this instance, as in many others, a broadness, a generosity, and a courage that commended him to all those who knew him, irrespective of faith or creed.

"While the bishop never had much money, yet he was always only too glad to share whatever he had with others, and even when he could afford larger outlays for himself, yet he always economised in everything that concerned his own personal comfort.

"The bishop was as much at home with the highest dignitaries of the Church or State, as he was sitting by the bedside of a poor, suffering fellow-creature in the humblest home. While he was as fond of a joke, and as full of fun as any one, he always required a strict observance of refinement and purity of thought, and could transform a weary, gloomy dinner party into a bright and cheerful gathering by some of his witty stories; or he could, by almost a single wave of his hand, change the tide of conversation and thought from what was low or vicious, to what might be helpful or uplifting. A friend tells the following story, as illustrating the bishop's fondness for fun, and yet, at the same time, abhorrence of anything that partook of vulgarity. On one occasion, in New York, at a large dinner at which the bishop was present, after the ladies had left the room, and the bishop and others had been reciting some amusing experiences, one gentleman suggested that as there were no ladies present, he had an experience to relate, whereupon the bishop with great politeness, but with equal dignity, requested that if it were a story that required the absence of ladies, he would be much obliged if the gentleman would consider him (the bishop) 'a lady' for the purpose of the occasion.

"This suggestion by the bishop was done so gracefully, and yet so quickly, that there was no interruption to the continuance of the pleasant gathering; and in fact, it was even more pleasant, for the reason that the bishop had fixed a standard of refinement for the wit and humour that stimulated every one present to their best efforts.

"While Bishop Wilmer had the gentleness of a dove, yet he had a 'lion's heart' and an 'eagle's eye.' If he ever had any uncontrollable fear of danger, he never showed it, and his only struggle seemed to be at times to avoid courting danger or being tempted into martyrdom which might seem ostentatious. Whenever there was a disagreeable duty to perform, or any matter came under consideration that made it seem disagreeable for an individual to act or assume a responsibility that might be dangerous, this rather remarkable man, either when a college boy or as the Bishop of Louisiana, was ever ready to act alone, or as follower, or leader. He never faltered in the face of danger, except to avoid being unduly conspicuous. He often said that martyrdom was so glorious that it was usually too great a temptation for some natures. On one occasion, when there was under discussion some action that involved a great deal of glory, as well as of risk, the bishop turned to those around him and spoke substantially as follows : 'Before we can decide our full duty in this matter we must eliminate as far as possible that glorious picture of martyrdom which may too often encourage us to deeds of heroism sometimes so selfish in their purpose.' Thus he discouraged useless effort, which, while it might have invited great public applause temporarily, yet was prompted almost wholly by a somewhat morbid desire for notoriety. The bishop aptly said, 'It is often a greater temptation to be a martyr, than to avoid the danger that might involve martyrdom.' Thus through his whole life there were evidences of a fearlessness which had been developed through a moral self-denial; and he proved, as few men prove, that the highest form of courage is that which results, not from an entire ignorance of fear, but from that control of fear which comes from training in methods of self-control. He knew no fear, not because he had never felt fear or because he had not passed through the timidity of childhood, but because, by reason of his purity and innocency of life, he had developed a conscience which could have no accuser.

"'A guilty conscience needs no accuser,' for its guilt is traceable to the conduct of its possessor, but a guiltless conscience comes from a purity and innocency of life that has shut out evil, and is consequently fearless of danger. Thus Bishop Wilmer's life exemplified what only such lives can exemplify, for he trained his life, his thoughts, and his feelings so that they were controlled alone by the highest motives and purposes.

Bishop Wilmer was a man of wide experience and close observation. While he was as pure-minded and innocent as a child, having carefully abstained from suspicious and cynical thoughts, as well as harmful associations, yet he thoroughly understood human nature, and was ever ready to meet any type of man; but he always used such an opportunity to try and direct the thoughts of his hearers and associates on lines that might be uplifting and helpful. He was ready alike to welcome the most guilty culprit or the most distinguished citizen, whenever he felt that such meeting might be productive of good; and he so trained himself to self-control by such high lines of thought that he was ever ready to know how to act in any emergency. He was naturally most cordial and genial in manner, yet he had that power of discrimination which fitted him to meet all men on the best terms.

" On one occasion, when visiting his son who was at a Northern college, they met a prominent man whom the son introduced to his father. As this gentleman had been very kind to young Wilmer, the young man was very cordial in his manner, and was somewhat disappointed and surprised to find that his father, the bishop, was rather cold and reserved. After the introduction, when the interview had closed, young Wilmer turned to his father and expressed great regret that the bishop had been somewhat undemonstrative and reserved, whereupon the bishop replied, 'Oh, my dear boy, when you are a little older, you will understand that the kindest hearts and the most cordial feelings are often hidden by a rather cold exterior. The gentleman who has been so kind to you, and whose kindness I deeply appreciate, does not belong to that class of men who at first understand demonstrativeness, or interpret it as you and I might wish. If I had treated him as I was inclined to do, it would have been unwelcome to him. He belongs to that class of people whose splendid natures have been reared up under influences that discourage all outward manifestations of feeling; and yet who may feel as deeply and sincerely as those of us who have been brought up in a different atmosphere. I appreciate, my dear boy, your desire that I should amply show my grateful feelings; but your friend, whom I now hope is my friend, understood more from my eye and the grasp of my hand, than he would have done from the most cordial or effusive expressions of gratitude. As you grow older, you will realise that human nature, while in the main it is alike in all people, yet, in different individuals, requires widely different treatment; and it may be a part of your study and experience in your college life, as well as hereafter, to learn how to discriminate between individuals.'

"Within a short time afterwards, young Wilmer met this aforesaid gentleman. He came up, and with surprising cordiality, spoke with unusual delight of the way in which the bishop had greeted him, and intimated his desire to see him again. It is needless to say that, as supplementing this impression, this same gentleman was ever afterward more kind and attentive to this college boy than ever before."

It would be impossible but that such incidents as a near kinsman has here recorded should have circulated in various forms and with slight differences. As a rule, of course, a son's recollections of his father must take foremost rank over any other recollections. But I am bound to say that, as I have originally heard it related, the bishop's visit to a Roman congregation, upon whom he urged patience and forbearance in a parish quarrel, was followed by a visit which he made to the pastor, who, it seems, had become intemperate. To him the bishop is said to have spoken with equal tenderness, wisdom, and fidelity. He disclaimed authority whether to reprove, rebuke, or exhort; but he plead, as one man with another, and crowned his plea with prayer. It is said that that pastor made it a turning-point in his life.

Two addresses to his Diocesan Convention, delivered by Bishop Wilmer, respectively in 1867 and 1868, have come into my hands. They help to complete this superficial portraiture of a personality of rare gifts and powers. The first of them closes with a discussion of the Race question in the South, which, though the words were uttered nearly forty years ago, is as true and as pertinent to-day as when the address was delivered. Bishop Wilmer, though born in New Jersey, was no Northern radical. He believed in the institution of slavery, while it existed, and made no pretence of satisfaction when it was abolished.

But, with the vision of a seer, he recognised, when the Civil War was ended, the new duties that had come to the South ; and in the address to which I have referred he pressed them home upon the Church people of Louisiana with rare eloquence, and with a splendid courage.

They are the same qualities which reveal themselves in his address of the following year. It was the year of the first Lambeth Conference, a gathering projected amid many doubts, and feeling its way with somewhat uncertain steps. But, however meagre its discussions or modest its output of declarations, Bishop Wilmer saw in it the dawn of a great purpose, and the promise of vast potentialities. That impressive movement toward Christian Unity which in the Lambeth Conference found its cradle, he recognised in its feeblest beginnings. With the larger discernment of a statesman he perceived "whereunto it might grow," and of what he saw, with characteristic eloquence, he spoke.

"The world affects" he said, "to sneer at Church councils as vain and useless. We have the authority of a great historian[1] for saying that the world is indebted to the Council of Nice for the first idea of a true representative assembly. The fact stands confessed that

[1] Alison, in his preface to the *History of Europe.*

nations have been taught how to rule and legislate for their subjects, by the example of the Church. A few years ago our American branch of the Church assembled in General Convention at the close of the war, to legislate for healing its wounds, and recovering the broken ties of ecclesiastical unity. In one day that task was completed. I am bold to say that if the civil power had been wise enough to work after that model, the peace of the Church would have been the peace of the Nation."

"This lesson is not yet completed," adds Bishop Wilmer. Nor is it, even now, we may frankly own. But as we do so, we must needs pay homage to the memory of one who, with inspired vision, beheld the day-dawn from afar!

Bishop Clarkson

VIII

𝔅ishop Clarkson

THE RIGHT REVEREND DR. ROBERT HARPER
CLARKSON, MISSIONARY BISHOP OF
NEBRASKA

THERE is a distinction in the nomencla-
ture obtaining in the American House of
Bishops which does not always seem quite real
or accurately descriptive. The bishops of what
are known as "organised dioceses" are designated, absolutely, as bishops, and have no
canonical responsibility (save that to the
General Convention, as the law-making body
for the whole Church) other than that to their
own diocese. The diocese elects them, assumes
the burden of their maintenance; and, as
organised under canonical provisions of the
General Convention, sits and votes, in the
persons of its representatives, in both Houses
of that body.

A "missionary bishop," on the other hand,
is a bishop chosen by the General Convention,

the House of Bishops nominating him, and the
House of (clerical and lay) Deputies electing
him—the two Houses voting separately,—and
is maintained by the Board of Missions.   He
has jurisdiction, usually, in one or more terri-
tories, or in some part of a territory, usually
but sparsely and newly settled, and where the
characteristics of frontier life—for usually it is
frontier life—are rude and primitive.   As a
matter of fact, however, the lot of a diocesan
bishop is often quite as austere and laborious.

It was to a missionary jurisdiction, including,
then, the whole of the territory of Nebraska,
that there was called, in 1865, the Rev. Dr.
Robert Harper Clarkson, at that time rector
of St. James's Church, Chicago; and no
episcopate in the American Church affords a
nobler illustration of the highest ideal of a
missionary bishop than did his.   Dr. Clarkson
was born, in 1826, at Gettysburg, Penn., of
churchly lineage; and those two facts were
singularly typical of much that was most distinctive in his character.   His grandfather, the
Rev. Dr. Joseph Clarkson, was the first
clergyman ordained by Bishop White; and
Robert Clarkson grew up among traditions
which were eminently conservative and retro-
spective in their character.   But when he went

The Right Reverend
Doctor Robert Harper Clarkson,
Missionary Bishop of Nebraska.
From a photograph by Notman & Campbell, Boston.

to Chicago, as a young priest, he must have
learned, if never before, why he had been born
in Gettysburg, and why life in the Church, like
life in the Republic, could not be merely a re-
affirmation of traditions in which his ancestors
had been nurtured.

In other words, he must early have learned—
what so nobly his episcopate illustrated—that
the work of the Church, and, incidentally, of a
bishop as a workman in it, did not, and could
not, consist in merely reproducing those
eminently respectable and decorous conventions
in which, at the beginning of the life of our
Republic, the life of the Church largely consisted. Young Clarkson went, upon his ordination, to Chicago, and became (in 1849) rector
of St. James's Church, there. The great city
which the more modern traveller knows was
then in its formless beginnings ; and its crude
construction, and especially its unwholesome
system of drainage,—if anything of that sort
could, then, have been said to exist,—made it a
prolific home for the awful scourge of cholera
which, almost before the young deacon,
Clarkson, was settled in his new home, began
its appalling ravages. These spared no class
or neighbourhood ; and, alas, too often the
ministers of religion, with others, fled before

it. But while others ran away, Clarkson never flinched.

"Day and night," as a Western newspaper put it, "the young deacon held his way among the stricken ; nursing the sick, helping the poor, cheering the hearts of the bereaved, holding the cross before the dying, and burying the forsaken dead. Stricken down, himself, he conquered the disease by his indomitable spirit ; and weak and weary as he was, went out, again, to the utter misery all around him, never stopping to rest ; never heeding the cries of fear." [1]

It can be easily imagined what a place such service won for him in the hearts of his fellow-citizens ; and how, as his work, and he himself, grew, in Chicago, his hold upon men of every class became stronger and more potential. Indeed, it would not have been surprising if, when he was elected a missionary bishop, he had returned answer that his duty was to stay in the city where he had begun his ministry, and where every problem that can challenge a minister of Christ was becoming so grave and so imperious. Other communities in the Republic, no matter how largely recruited from abroad, have seemed to inherit, and to have retained, some of those conservative elements which have helped to maintain, and continue in healthful efficacy, earlier standards of

[1] *Omaha Herald*, March 11, 1884.

dignity and order. New York, for instance, polyglot as it is, and vast as are the hordes of aliens that have continued to pour into it, has not yet lost—Heaven grant that it may never lose !—the potent spell of those earlier Dutch traditions which, from the beginning of its civic life, have been such efficient forces on the side of civic order and righteousness. But Chicago, whatever estimable qualities may have distinguished its New England founders, speedily passed into the hands of elements so mixed, and, in many characteristics, so revolutionary, that no civic upheaval occurring there, whether at the polls, or in the streets, has greatly surprised men.

To such a community it is not difficult to imagine what such a man as Dr. Robert Clarkson might have been ; and to leave it for the work of a frontiersman in Nebraska must needs have seemed, to many dispassionate minds, a very doubtful duty.

But it did not seem so to Dr. Clarkson. Personally, he had every inducement to decline the call of the General Convention to Nebraska. The town to which he had gone as a young deacon had grown to the proportions of a wealthy and populous community; and the little wooden edifice in which, originally, he

had ministered, had given place to a stately
and beautiful stone structure, distinguished in
all its appointments by cost and splendour.
Better than all this, Dr. Clarkson's influence
had grown with his own years, and with the
intelligent appreciation of the character of his
ministry; and few men have ever lived in
Chicago who have touched with a hand so
sympathetic and inspiring the lives of men, and
especially of young men.　What was there in
Nebraska to compare with a centre of such influence and power? There is abundant evidence
that questions such as this were pressed home
upon him, when the call to Nebraska came to
him; but he did not refuse it.　It had come to
him from the whole Church, by the voice of its
General Convention; and though, as Bishop
Hare says, in his memorial sermon, "the
announcement [of his election] drove the blood
from his cheeks and left him speechless for
moments," he could not disown its authority.
In a sermon preached to his people in St.
James's Church, Chicago, announcing his decision, he used these words:

"Entirely unexpected, without the slightest desire on
my part, and with scarcely the shadow of training, the
announcement of the Church came upon me.　The very
thought of the necessary severing of ties, and disturbing

of the associations of seventeen years of a happy pastorate, was more than I could bear. And whilst I was enduring anguish and agitation in the balancing of inclination with duty, such as I pray God I may never again experience, I went to one of the bishops, and told him that I could not and would not go, and laid before him the reasons for my decision,—ultimate as I then thought it. When I told him of my ministry here, commenced in the fervour and enthusiasm of youth, and deep-rooted in the spiritual services and pastoral experiences of so many years,—of my flock united in a most remarkable degree, and precious to me, every one, without an exception, and of my delightful home, filled with numberless testimonials of your attachment,—and of my beautiful church, every stone of which was cemented by my anxieties and my prayers,—and of the city with which I had grown up, the only dwelling place of my manhood's years, the birthplace of my children, and the sleeping ground of my dead—I supposed that this was enough to satisfy any reasonable man that I ought not to be asked to go. His only reply, as he laid his hand upon my shoulder, and looked me calmly in the eye, was: 'Your Master in heaven left infinitely more than this for you. Life is short. The account you must give will be strict. Go where He has sent you.' What could I say? Shame and silence sealed my lips. From that hour the more I thought over the matter, and the more I prayed over it, and the more I discussed it with holy men, who believe that there is a God, and that there are such things as duty, accountability, necessary self-surrender, and the baptism of the Holy Ghost, the clearer grew the whole subject, the more insignificant and sinful seemed the thought of the personal sacrifice

9

involved, and the more imperative became the demand
of conscience; and, although I reserved the right of final
decision until I came home, and did not definitely de-
termine until since my return, yet every day has settled
me firmer in the conviction best expressed in the lines
of the text, 'What am I that I could withstand God?'"

It was with such a conception of his duty
that Bishop Clarkson turned his back upon his
great city parish, and went forth to the wilderness and its privations. Men—and things—
move so fast in America that, already, it is not
easy to realise what a Western territory was in
the year 1865. Nebraska is already a great,
state, gridironed with railways and dotted,
from end to end, with thriving towns. Then
it was a wilderness with, here and there, a
settlement of log-cabins, or of clap-board
houses, poor, perishable, and, often, pathetically significant. For, whether the Nebraskan
settler came from New England, New York,
or beyond seas, he came, ordinarily, under
stern compulsion, with narrow means, and
meagre outfit, and only an equipment of the
"larger hope."

Indeed, it is one of the painful conditions of
a missionary episcopate in the United States
that it is, so often, a service where the bond-
man is called upon, like the Hebrew slaves in

Egypt, to "make bricks without straw." A
missionary field in which the objects of the
Church's care are savages has, at any rate, this
advantage, that they to whom the missionary
is sent have no impossible expectations in
regard to himself, or his chapel. If the one
be the least cultivated of men, and the other
the simplest of structures, both are far in
advance of anything of either sort that the
savage has known. But a missionary bishop
in our far West has often ministered to people
of inherited refinement, and of liberal culture.
If one had time to listen to their ancestral
traditions, these were found, often, to run back
to refined homes, and stately sanctuaries, and
scholarly ministries, far away ; the memories of
which were but a poor preparation for the
privations of the life of a backwoodsman.
And so it came to pass that the bishop had,
often, to listen to the complaints of a flock who
forgot—to use a vulgar proverb—that "one
cannot secure all the moral virtues for a
shilling a day"—or, in other words, that a
Western missionary, barely keeping body and
soul together on a stipend that did not often
reach a thousand dollars a year, could not be
expected to illustrate the wide culture and
intellectual superiority that were within the

reach, alone, of men of more scholarly opportunities and ampler resources. " Our minister
is so dull, so crude, so unlettered, so poorly
endowed !" complained these rural congrega-
tions to the bishop. And the bishop, instead
of resenting these utterly unreasonable demands as they deserved, would simply reply,
" Oh, well ; next time I will send you the
Archbishop of Canterbury !"

It was this inexhaustible and exuberant
cheerfulness and good temper · that was no
small element of the power of Bishop Clarkson.
" He was, as a boy," says Bishop Hare, in the
memorial sermon to which I have already referred, "just what those of us who knew him
only as a man, would have inferred,—full of
life and spirits ; susceptible to every impression
from without ; endowed with a keen sense of
the ludicrous ; and hungry for all sorts of fun."
Happy gift, that, all the way through, kept his
heart young, and made life for him a less
sombre and irksome thing, because, so often,
he could transfix its most vexatious experiences with the Ithuriel spear of humour!
Said the late Dr. Clinton Locke, at that time
rector of Grace Church, Chicago, speaking at a
memorial service held in St. James's Church,
Chicago, after the bishop's death, of the

visits that Bishop Clarkson was wont to make
to him :

"He never complained of anything that he had to
endure ; and, with that brightness which was so
characteristic of him, turned every discomfort into a
source of amusement ; but he could tell a story of trials
and perils, by land and water, by flood and tempest, by
heat and cold, during the early years of his episcopate in
Nebraska and Dakota, which would shock the nerves of
many a man who thinks himself hardly used if he has
to pass one night away from all the appliances of modern
civilisation."

And yet, such elements in his work he threw
aside with the utter disregard of features of
hardship which was invariably characteristic
of him. He had but just entered the House of
Bishops when I first knew him ; but though I
then observed him with all the intense admiration of youth for his ripe heroism ; and though,
not then a bishop myself, I listened with eager
respect and enthusiasm for his stories of his
work and his office, I never heard him utter
even in any of the most confidential discussions
in that House, one word of recital which in
anywise implied the note of hardship or privation in his experiences ; though from others I
learned how much there was of both. His
characteristics in the House of Bishops were
those of great mental alertness, modesty, and

invariable and universal kindliness. There
were men sitting beside him in that body from
whom his own ecclesiastical training—and
theirs—made him, inevitably, far removed.
But no one would have ever discovered such a
fact in anything in his speech or bearing. He
understood with a fine discernment his own
intellectual limitations ; and did not commit the
blunder which is, so often, the blunder of the
theologian, of mistaking intellectual limitations
in others for moral obliquity.

A great bishop, referring to the episcopate
of another whose administration of his diocese
had singularly failed to fulfil the anticipations
which had been formed of it, said that similar
failures had led him to apprehend that a very
successful parish priest would rarely make an
efficient bishop ; and, when asked to explain
so occult an observation, answered that a very
successful parish priest was, ordinarily, an ab-
solutist ; that the government of his parish
was, usually, a paternal government ; and that
the principle of a paternal, as distinguished
from a constitutional, government was that it
was " rule without reasons," — the exercise of
authority without the elements of conference
and consultation ; and that while, for obvious
reasons, it was possible to govern a parish in

that way, it was a fatal blunder to attempt so to administer a diocese.

Obviously : for a diocese is ordinarily made up of men many of whom regard themselves as, in mental endowments and ecclesiastical experience, quite the peer of their bishop ; while with all of them there is a keen sensitiveness to constitutional rights and dignities, which makes them swift to resent, in the Ordinary, any even apparent disregard of them. In these respects Bishop Clarkson's administration was ideal. He was undoubtedly much more than the peer of the great majority of his clergy. But he never forgot that magnificent law of episcopal service which, the Rev. Dr. Samuel Hart tells us, in his noble sermon, memorial of the fourth bishop of Connecticut, Bishop Williams, when he began his journal as bishop, wrote at the head of it : " If thou be made the master, lift not thyself up, but be among them as one of the rest."[1] Bishop Clarkson never forgot that rule ; and, because he worked *with*, as well as *for*, his clergy and his diocese (as it speedily came to be), the Church in Nebraska grew from its feeble beginnings into a noble ripeness and maturity.

I may well conclude these recollections of

[1] Ecclesiasticus xxxii., 1.

Bishop Clarkson by a tribute to his memory
paid by a citizen of Nebraska at a meeting of
the citizens of Omaha, held in Boyd's Opera
House on the evening of the 12th of March,
1884. This meeting was the more remarkable
in that it included, in those who took part in
it, people of all nationalities and walks in life,
and of all communions. It was a citizens'
meeting, to honour one who had never forgotten the duties of his office, but had made
that office larger and more potential than
its merely ecclesiastical traditions. Mr. Poppleton [1] spoke as follows :

" Bishop Clarkson first visited Omaha in December,
1865, and shortly after became a permanent resident.
At that time Omaha had just become fully aroused from
the lethargy which had settled upon it in September,
1857, and seemed girding itself for the growth and prosperity which these latter years have witnessed. The
territory was slowly recovering from a prolonged stagna-
tion in immigration and development, which had driven
many from its borders, and discouraged and disheart-
ened those at home. There were less than fifty miles of
railway in Nebraska. The extension of that was doubtful and uncertain. Many of the great railway systems
which have during his residence among us gradually
extended themselves west of the Missouri until their
mileage is reckoned by thousands, and no federal territory is left untouched, were unorganised and unknown.

[1] The Hon. A. J. Poppleton.

"The vast territory constituting his missionary jurisdiction was rich in nothing but natural resources, and in the hearts and arms of widely scattered settlements, led largely by men under forty years of age, who had by accident or impulse effected a lodgment in that particular spot, and with their homes and altars were there to stay. To the vision of those who for years had waited for the dawn, the future seemed as gloomy as the past; and they looked forward rather with anxiety than hope.

"Coming to the territory at such a time, Bishop Clarkson made an enormous contribution to the hope and confidence of the people. Victor Hugo says of one of his ideal heroes, 'He was one, but he was equal to ten thousand!' With a quick, keen sympathy which seemed to touch every phase of life, he identified himself in feeling and act with all worthy plans for material growth and progress. With a never flagging hope, inspired, perhaps, to some extent by the marvellous progress of the city from which he came, and a clear vision of the latent possibilities of the empire through which his journeyings led, he was a living force in the advancement of every enterprise.

"Some of us, too, remember that when any long-watched work had been crowned with success, and we gathered together fitly to celebrate its completion, he was often present, one of the chief contributors to the instruction and happiness of the occasion. These things, without impairing in the slightest degree his official character or influence, brought him near to thousands of business men and people who held no church relations.

"Probably the general body of the people of Omaha has never contributed so liberally to any one religious

enterprise, as to the beautiful cathedral which was his
last and crowning work, — fit monument to his memory.
How much of this was due to the universal respect and
regard begotten of his deep interest in the general prosperity and growth of the city of his residence !

" The highest attribute of citizenship is patriotism.
The scholar who preferred poverty and toil in his own
country, to wealth and a title of nobility on condition of
expatriation, gave to the world one of its noblest ex-
amples of human virtue.   Bishop Clarkson lived in
times which intensified his natural love for his country.
He saw nothing in his ecclesiastical office to divorce
him from the duties of citizenship.   He was master of
the history and frame of the government, and to him
his country was a living presence.   It was not in his
nature to hate anything ; but he believed in the sover-
eignty and supremacy of the federal government within
its sphere, and he accepted with all his heart every act
and construction necessary to maintain it inviolate.   He
saw, as all clear sighted men see, that upon no other
foundation could a permanent nationality rest ; and it
was doubtless one of the felicities of his life, that he
lived to see the great North American Republic at
peace upon the only question which ever menaced its
existence.

" Nebraska has attained a population of perhaps seven
hundred thousand people.[1]   It has made unexampled
strides in prosperity.   It has railways, mills, banks,
herds, farms, and the ten thousand forms of material
wealth.   All these things are constantly increasing.   The
greed for wealth, sharpened by indulgence, but never
satisfied by acquisition, seldom actually curbed by any

[1] This was the population of Nebraska in 1884.

moral restraint, expands its deathly foliage over the citizen, the family, and the State—until many of the best people come to believe, or live as if they believed, the husks of life were its fruit and flower. The character of the State is in the moral, intellectual, and spiritual exaltation of its people. The deathless memories of the earth are not of cash accumulations, but of heroic deeds, glorified spirits, intellectual conquests, sacrifices of men's selves, education, refinement, culture, moral, intellectual, and spiritual exaltation. His faultless taste, his sympathetic eloquence, his simple manners, his pervading charity, his contagious sympathy, left every community he visited wiser, nobler, and better than he found it."

Bishop Brooks

IX

𝕭𝖎𝖘𝖍𝖔𝖕 𝕭𝖗𝖔𝖔𝖐𝖘

THE RIGHT REVEREND DR. PHILLIPS BROOKS,
BISHOP OF MASSACHUSETTS

THE Reverend Dr. Phillips Brooks, rector of Trinity Church, Boston, was consecrated Bishop of Massachusetts on October 14, 1891. He died on January 23, 1893. In other words, his episcopate was only little more than fifteen months in length. He sat in only one General Convention, and that the convention held in Baltimore in October, 1892. There would be little, therefore, to be told of his life as a bishop, under any circumstances ; and, in his case, there was the less, because deliberative bodies of any sort but slightly interested him, and ecclesiastical deliberative bodies least of all. I shall hope, therefore, to be indulged, if, before I recall the brief recollections which I have to rehearse of his later years, I speak of my earlier knowledge of him, when he and I were students together, and reproduce, in these pages, some memories of singular felicity and discernment written for a clerical club in Boston, soon after his death, by his close and gifted friend, the Rev. Dr. Charles A. L. Richards.

Phillips Brooks entered the Theological Seminary of Virginia in the autumn of 1856. At that time the seminary was overcrowded, not only the main building (of which there is an admirable picture in the Rev. Dr. A. V. G. Allen's *Life and Letters of Phillips Brooks*, and which has, long since, disappeared) but another called " St. John's in the Wilderness," occupied by the students, and buried among the trees that, before the Civil War, crowned the seminary hill, being filled to the top. It was to the top that young Brooks, whose height approximated to six feet and four inches, was relegated; and, when I found him there, he could not stand up straight. Nearly thirty years after, when I had become Bishop of New York, at an alumni dinner of the Virginia Seminary, Dr. Brooks told the story of his extrication from that dilemma, and concluded with expressing "the hope that Henry Potter would continue to help men to stand up straight"; as, he might have added, St. Paul

The Right Reverend Doctor Phillips Brooks,
Bishop of Massachusetts.
From the engraving by A. B. Hall.

had done at Lystra (Acts xiv., 10). In the *Impressions of Phillips Brooks*, by Dr. Richards, to which I have already referred, the writer tells the story of that somewhat monastic life to which a young school-teacher who had not found it his vocation to govern unruly boys turned, when he recognised his call to the ministry. It cannot be pretended that he found in the Virginia Seminary a congenial intellectual atmosphere. By a fortunate coincidence, he enjoyed, there, the friendship of two men,—Charles A. L. Richards and George A. Strong, who were, all his life long, perhaps his closest friends, and whose wide culture and scholarly tastes were to him like a draught of cool water to parched lips. But, otherwise, the atmosphere in which he found himself in Virginia was quite unlike that which he had left behind him in Massachusetts; and the great majority of his fellow-students in the seminary, instead of admiring, or appreciating, his varied reading and classical culture, accounted both as notes of a somewhat pagan ideal of learning.

On the other hand, the narrow routine of a pietistic life, in the midst of which he found himself at the seminary, must have been equally surprising and perplexing to the young

graduate of Harvard.   Most of all, the physical hardships and privations of his Virginia
student life, to one who had been nurtured
amid the less casual and more orderly characteristics of New England housekeeping
must have been irritating and distasteful.
Other men, bred as he had been, could not
endure them; and I remember very well a
New Englander, who afterwards in his ministry, both as priest and bishop, won high
distinction, who was reported to have left the
seminary and gone elsewhere for his theological training, because the beds were so hard!
But I cannot recall a single reference, on
Brooks's part, to any of these things, that was
other than playful.   He refused to regard
them seriously; and, though, as Dr. Allen's
biography of him shows, he wrote his father
of what he thought the unsatisfactory character of the teaching of the institution, as not
realising his ideal of wide and varied scholarship, he early discerned, beneath its superficial
aspects whether material or intellectual, the
reality of that life which, for the Christian
student, or minister, is of pre-eminent importance,—the life that is spiritual.

Indeed, I am tempted at this point to insist
perhaps with more emphasis than have any of

his biographers upon the enduring value of his seminary life. A nature so intellectually and emotionally intense as his could not have been reared merely amid choicer intellectual environments, without the benumbing of sympathies which, later, flowered into such rare service for God and man. What he was in Philadelphia, and, later, whether as rector or bishop, in Boston, he was, in part at any rate, because his ministerial training had begun in Virginia. And yet, when that training was ended, and he went to his parish in Pennsylvania, he did not at the beginning, at any rate, reveal the power that was in him. Says the Rev. Dr. Richards in the " Remembrances " to which I have already referred :

"At the first of his ministry in Philadelphia the fame of Henry Wise, with his cadaverous look, his burning eyes, his Southern intensity of manner, his rare facility of speech, quite overshadowed any later comer in the field. Brooks told me once, that, exchanging with Wise, he found himself among the congregation after the service was over and heard a neighbour say : 'You wouldn't have caught me here to-night if I had not thought to hear Wise.' Brooks, not at all the traditional sort of eloquent divine, at first failed of recognition. Gradually people came to see that this tall young fellow, whom the great Dr. Vinton so often asked to preach for him, was head and shoulders above his brethren in something more than stature; that he had a message for ears that knew how to hear, and that he had no occasion to shelter himself behind Ward Beecher's maxim that 'everything must be young before it is old; and therefore Providence permits young ministers.' I can hear, now, Dr. Vinton's deep voice with a tone of surprise in it, after one of those sermons in the dusk of a winter afternoon in that great church, as he said with conviction, 'Why, he's an orator.' It gave Brooks, in his modest way, keen pleasure to be invited, later, when he was called to the Church of the Holy Trinity, to succeed Dr. Vinton, the pastor of his boyhood in St. Paul's, Boston, an unmistakable king of men, who loomed up in the eyes of one trained under his preaching into even more than his actual proportions. When the flattering call came it was declined. Presently, with urgency, it was repeated. Mr. Brooks, the elder, hastened to the scene, with natural parental alarm at his son's being thrust into a place of such responsibility. Aware of my familiar acquaintance with Phillips, he asked me what I thought of it. I told him I had no question of Brooks's abundant ability for that or any other pulpit; but I was anxious lest the quantity of work in so large a field might overtax him. With a look of relief, he replied, 'If you will answer for his brains, I will answer for all the rest of him. He never found anything hard in his life.' I sometimes suspect that he never did, to the very last of it. There was never any apparent effort, no matter what load was laid upon him. He worked not merely with a will, but without friction. He was at my house, once, on Thursday in Holy Week, a little fagged with the Lenten labours. He was to preach on Good Friday morning, make an address to his people in the afternoon, talk to the soldiers at a hospital Saturday noon, and have a preparatory lecture Saturday evening, preach on Easter Day, morning and night, and have a talk to his Sunday School between times. And nothing of it all was ready. The days of 'hustlers' in the ministry were not yet; and to my inexperienced vision the prospect was appalling. But he was as serene as midsummer. The half-dozen sermons and addresses fell into line as the season came for each; and each did its work efficiently. I took pains to inquire of those who heard him. And this was in his early ministry."

And it was characteristic of his later ministry also. Indeed, it was one of the mysteries, to some of those who knew and loved him best, who sympathised with his "point of view," and turned with a joy equal to his to the tasks which he and they were called to do, that he could face them always so cheerily; and that, behind the man's tasks, as, steadily, as his years ripened, they grew and greatened, there was always the boy's heart, revealing itself in a certain glad exuberance, even when he found himself face to face with the tremendous burdens of the episcopate. To the friend from whose "Remembrances" I have been quoting, he writes on the eve of his consecration :

"Yes, the bishops have consented, and I am to be consecrated on Wednesday, the 14th of October, in Trinity Church, Boston. You will come, won't you? You have seen me through so much of life that I am sure you will

not refuse me this, and I promise not to be made anything else as long as I live.

"When I think how much of other people's thoughts
I have dared to occupy for the last three months, I am
truly ashamed of myself ; but it has not been my fault.
And now it is over, and I shall go into the upper house,
and be forgotten.

"I have been visiting Arthur : next week I go for a
few days to John. I feel like Jephthah's daughter on
her round of farewell visits, and as if I were never going
to see anybody any more. On my way to Arthur I
stopped and saw Bishop ———, who was kind, and
talked as if he had always known that I could say the
Apostles' and Nicene Creeds, and had wanted me in the
House of Bishops from the start."

And then the last lines of December 29,
1892 :

"I spent the Feast of the Nativity with Arthur. One
of the strange things about the new place" (he means
the bishop's place) "is that one is freest on the days
which used to be the least free. Nobody wants a bishop
on Christmas or Good Friday. So Arthur took me in,
and I preached for him morning and afternoon. William
and his family went on, also, and we had a big family
dinner on Monday evening, and played childish games
till midnight ; and it was all very simple, and silly, and
delightful. I did not stay for the cathedral corner-
stone. I like to do my pageants in Chicopee, and Van
Deusenville : New York is far too big and bumptious ;
Potter may have that to himself."

In concluding his "Remembrances" Dr.

Richards sums up his impressions of Bishop Brooks in sentences that are marked by a singularly impartial and acute discernment :

" Brooks was not a profound scholar. He was well grounded in his classics, and full of the spirit of the ancient masters in literature, but I think rarely reverted to the Greek and Latin writers. He read French with delight. Its lucidity was congenial to him. He read German with some facility. He was a wide reader, but by no means an omnivorous reader in his own tongue. I do not think he was familiar with the earlier English writers, or with the modern German scholars, as Washburn, for example, was. Of late years he had small time for reading, yet he was always well abreast of current thought, and knew whatever was most worth while in literature. He was not a constructive theologian. Religious thought did not assume a dogmatic shape with him. I do not know that he can be called a great, or original, thinker. I say this hesitatingly, for I am aware others differ from me. Yet it might be difficult to point out in his published volumes, any leading thought which could not be traced to older sources in Arnold and Whately, in Robertson, Maurice and Stanley, in McLeod Campbell, and Horace Bushnell. He was not a great organiser of institutions. They sprang up under his impulse, but others shaped them. He rather under-valued the administrative men, thought they made too much of their convenient and serviceable gift, and were ranked higher in the common esteem than the occasion called for. He was not a fiery champion of causes or leader of multitudes, like Wesley or Luther. His words were not half battles, like Luther's. They were victorious marches across the field. They were serene influences,

filling the air like sunshine. Men breathed them as
health into their lungs. Personally, he was a great
character. Intellectually, we might call him a genius of
the highest order in the application of the good news of
Christ to everyday, modern life. His distinction and
originality were there.

" Others have shared his profound faith and broad,
inclusive love ; but who has had such buoyancy of hope
as he ? such sublime confidence that all must come
right in God's own world, which Jesus was born in and
died for, where the Holy Spirit was a deathless presence
and power ? Partly it was a native endowment, partly it
had been developed by the rare happiness of his life ;
but it was a Christian grace also, cultivated through
seasons of anxiety and of sorrow, ripened by experience
of what good things God had wrought. The young
were drawn to him, as to one who, in this as in so much
else, never ceased to be a boy, and the old retricked
their beams, and found ' glad, confident morning ' again.
It was a hopefulness that did not make him rash or pre-
sumptuous, but only glad and humble, and calmly ex-
pectant ; sure of God's great purpose and tender mercy,
sure that man was able to hold countless treasures from
the divine influx ; sure that God was ever reaching out
towards the accomplishment of his ideal for humanity
once revealed to us in Jesus Christ. All things were at
work for his good, our good, all men's good, and what
glories were in reserve so soon as we loved the Lord
Jesus ! It was a hope so strong and vital as at times to
seem unreasoning. Leave God out of the premises, it
was indeed unreasonable. But holding to Him, anchored
within the veil, it had a right to be, and never fog could
damp, nor storm could shake it.

"Bishop Brooks, as I have said, was rarely fortunate in his life ; in his native gifts, his home influences, his early associations, the occasions and opportunities that were opened to him. The vicissitudes of the few years of our national struggle, at the outset of his ministry, developed and educated him ; the conflict with slavery intensified his manhood ; the new movement in theology made room for him, stimulated his intellect, and broadened his range. He grew in New England as a strong tree in congenial soil. The passing storms or droughts only sent the roots deeper and gave them firmer foothold. Under his widespread boughs how large a flock at last found shelter ! "

As I began by saying, Bishop Brooks's episcopate was very brief ; but not so brief as to be without significant and suggestive notes. One may venture to affirm, now, what no record of his life has seen fit quite candidly to recognise,—that there cannot be the smallest doubt that, toward the end of his life, his mind underwent a fundamental change as to the episcopate. He was a man of ideas; and, as such, he did not greatly value institutions. He gloried in "the living creature within the wheels,"—for the wheels, themselves, he did not greatly care; and of this he made no secret. His prophetic office, as a preacher, he regarded as the highest of all the ministerial callings; and he regarded bishops, usually,

with a good-natured condescension which did
not trouble itself to understand their office, or
to appreciate its influence. In all this, he was
seconded by a chorus of divines, who were
careful never to contradict him, and who, in
this glorification of the preacher's office, caught
the reflected lustre of their own. It was to
these adoring followers a rude blow when they
found that their idol was willing to be a
bishop,—nay, not only willing, but anxious ;
and they looked into one another's faces with
a dismay which found no alleviation in the
sphinx-like silence of their leader.

But upon the mind of their leader there
had broken, late and slowly, a new light. He
came to see that, in the episcopate, one might
find the largest opportunity for the largest
powers. He came to see that what he had
reckoned a calling of dry routine might be
transformed—and that with no violent dis-
memberment of its component parts—into a
ministry of noblest opportunities and of most
potential service. And nothing is finer in his
whole history than the frankness with which,
when once he discerned this, he set about realising it. I have referred, elsewhere,[1] to the
sublime reticence with which, during the time

[1] See in *Law and Loyalty*, p. 263, a sermon preached at the consecration of Phillips Brooks.

that elapsed between his election to the episcopate, and his consecration as Bishop of Massachusetts, he endured in an heroic silence, and
with uncomplaining patience, the attacks which,
from so many quarters, were hurled at him by
fellow-Churchmen because of what was alleged
to be his doctrinal unsoundness.   But, in truth
this was but a part of that nobler whole which
disclosed itself after he became a bishop.   As a
presbyter he had not been over-careful about
rubrics, canons, and the rest, and there was
undoubtedly a considerable contingent among
those who had, until his consecration, been his
fellow-presbyters, who looked to see him illustrate in his episcopate a fine disdain for laws
and forms.   But, if they did, they were doomed
to be woefully disappointed.   From the time
that Bishop Brooks turned his face toward
the episcopal office, he saw, as though it had
broken upon him in a strong light, that the
office of religion is both inspirational *and* organic ;—that there cannot be life in the divine society, without the incarnation of that life;
and that the moment one has gotten that far,
the inevitable necessity that the life organic
must be a life of law, of rule, of related forces,
—of authority, in one word,—and of obedience,
becomes overwhelmingly clear.

It is from this point of view that the brief episcopate of Bishop Brooks derives the highest lustre.   His predecessors, and especially that one
whom he immediately followed, had been men
who had found, in canon law, an imperative
voice; and when Bishop Brooks succeeded
them, the world looked to see this man of
genius, this preacher of inspired power treat
all homage for red-tape with large contempt.
As a matter of fact, they saw nothing of the
sort.   Never was there a sublimer illustration
of these words of the centurion captain, " I also
am a man set under authority, having under
me soldiers."[1]   He vindicated his right to rule,
by his readiness to obey.   He recognised that,
under a constitutional form of government,
such as that of the Church, there cannot be
anything save anarchy, unless they who administer the law obey it ; and his obedience was as
scrupulous as it was cheerful.

But he did not love lawmaking, and he did not
pretend to.   In the only General Convention
in which he sat he was one of the junior bishops;
and his place, as such, in the House of Bishops,
was near the door.   I was going out of it, one
day when, as I passed his seat, he plucked my
sleeve and, drawing me down, whispered in my
ear, " Henry, *is it always as dull as this?*"

[1] St. Luke vii., 8.

It was inevitable that, to him, the House of
Bishops should be dull. As a newcomer,
there, he was expected to be silent; and as
a listener he could hope only to hear rather
dry discussions concerning terms and phrases
in which he could find little to interest him.
But the fine feature in that whole situation consisted in his scrupulous attendance, and in his
painstaking attention. Parliamentary techni-
calities, canonical amendments, titular designa-
tions and distinctions, in no wise appealed to
him. But he followed the business of the
House with scrupulous vigilance, and—with
one exception—in unbroken silence.

That exception had in it a note of such
absolute simplicity and almost boyish enthusiasm that I cannot but recall it.

We were listening to the report of the joint
committee on the Hymnal. Originally, as
some of my readers will remember, there was,
bound up with the Prayer Book, a metrical version of certain psalms, and a selection of hymns,
little more than two hundred in number and of
very variable quality. It had been decided to
substitute for these a proper Hymnal; and the
best talent in the Church had, for two or three
General Conventions, and for the years between them, devoted itself, bishops, presbyters,

and laymen, to the preparation of this Hymnal. At last the work was completed; and, after considerable previous discussion, the committee submitted the book in the House of Bishops for its final adoption.

Until this time, Bishop Brooks had not, so far as I can remember, opened his lips in the House of Bishops. But, as the chairman of the joint committee on the Hymnal sat down, the bishop rose, with his characteristic modesty, and spoke in substance as follows:

" One can readily understand, and heartily sympathise with, many of the changes in our collection of hymns of which the able report of the joint committee is the evidence. There is a most gratifying enlargement of the old collection, and some hymns which obviously were scarcely worthy of a place in it have disappeared. But a hymn has two values, one of which is doctrinal, and the other literary, and added to these is that often mightiest power which comes from association. I venture to submit, Mr. Chairman, that that last is pre-eminently true of the hymn beginning ' How firm a foundation, ye saints of the Lord.' "

And along that line the Bishop of Massachusetts spoke with great tenderness and power. He made no high claim for the hymn on the ground of its literary merits; but he dwelt with persuasive earnestness upon its very sacred associations with the deepest life of

individual believers ; and concluded by expressing his regret that the committee had seen fit
to omit it, and he then made a motion that it
be restored.

As he sat down, there sprang to his feet a
bishop who had most vehemently opposed his
confirmation, and who was generally reckoned
to have been the most active foe to his admission to the House of Bishops. With impassioned
eloquence, he seconded the motion of the
Bishop of Massachusetts, and expressed, with
vehement speech, his delight in doing so, and
his hearty concurrence with every argument
that the bishop had used. Without further
debate the vote was taken on the resolution,
and carried by a large majority ; and the hymn
(No. 636) may be found to-day in the episcopal
Hymnal.

Its author, as some who read these words
may remember, was Keen, not like Neale,
Wesley, Toplady, Watts, Frances Havergal, or
others, famous for hymn writing, or otherwise.
But the hymn is interwoven with the child-life
of many devout men, and, as doubtless was the
case in this instance, with memories of a
sainted mother. And who shall say what
thoughts awoke in the breast of this man of
genius who combined the splendour of rare gifts

with a singularly simple and child-like faith, as he plead for that grand old hymn? Sacred were the lips that once had taught it. Imperishable was the faith that, at a mother's knee, had learned it!

Bishop Dudley

161

X

𝔅𝔦𝔰𝔥𝔬𝔭 𝔇𝔲𝔡𝔩𝔢𝔶

THE RIGHT REVEREND DR. THOMAS UNDERWOOD
DUDLEY, BISHOP OF KENTUCKY

IN a charge to the Diocese of Virginia delivered in 1904 or 1905, the Bishop of that
Diocese, the Right Reverend Robert A. Gibson, D. D., refers to the various causes and
influences that have led men to turn their faces
toward the ministry ; and alludes especially to
the considerable number of men who at the
close of the Civil War, both in the North and
in the South, gave themselves to that calling.

There can be no doubt about the fact, nor
as to the striking illustrations of it which are
afforded by the history of the American Episcopate. In the arrangement of seats in the
House of Bishops the juniors sit in the rear;
and I can remember very well when, at the
last General Convention in which I was acting
as secretary of the House of Bishops, and, as
such, assigning seats and desks to the newly

consecrated bishops, I found four of them sitting in close proximity to each other, every one of whom had been an officer in the Confederate service. Turning to that one of them who happened to be nearest to me I said, "Gentlemen, I think I shall have to nail up a copy of the United States flag in this corner of the House!" Whereupon dear Harris, then Bishop of Michigan, promply responded, "Go ahead! We can stand it—if you can!"

Such an incident explained the action of many noble men, and of Bishop Dudley among them. He was a typical Southerner; and, to the last, he never lost those distinctive qualities of speech, of temperament, of character, which have so greatly endeared him, and hosts of other Southerners, to their more frigid brethren of the North. His large vision and rare practical wisdom restrained him from merely impulsive and emotional action; but no one who knew him could be uncertain as to the strong fires of deep affection, of high purpose, and of unbending devotion to duty that glowed beneath all that he did. United to these qualities, moreover, there was an altogether unusual gift of scholarship, which made of him the distinguished Grecian that he was in college, and, later, the enthusiastic disciple

The Right Reverend
Doctor Thomas Underwood Dudley
Bishop of Kentucky
From a photograph by Nagell.

The Right Reverend
Doctor Thomas Underwood Dudley,
Bishop of Kentucky.
From a photograph by Naegeli.

of that rare thinker, Dr. William Sparrow, at whose feet he sat in the Theological Seminary of Virginia.

Bishop Dudley was born on September 26, 1837, in Richmond, Virginia, and his ancestry bound him to that illustrious Commonwealth by ties that were never broken. It was natural that the 'son of such a lineage should be entered in due time at the University of Virginia, and he was graduated there in 1858. From Dr. L. M. Blackford, now the Principal of the Episcopal High School of Virginia, which is situated some three miles west of Alexandria, and not far from the Theological Seminary of Virginia, I have been so fortunate as to secure the following letter:

". . . The late Bishop Dudley and I, being about the same age, entered the University of Virginia together in October, 1855, and we were intimate there as well as ever after. We had never met before entering the University, so that I am unable to give you any information as to his *school* life. I remember that he came to college direct from the Hanover Academy, Va., of which Lewis M. Coleman, M. A., was head master, a noted academy in those days. Coleman afterwards became professor of Latin in the University, and, later, a colonel of artillery in the Confederate service, in which he died, in the Battle of Fredericksburg. Dudley was particularly fond of him and Coleman was proud of his distinguished pupil, at whose graduation in 1858 he was present; for I remember seeing him congratulate Dudley's parents on that occasion, in the public hall.   Dudley's earlier training was at a day school in Richmond. "

It will not be inappropriate, though they extend over a much longer period, to follow these reminiscences from one college classmate to those of another, Dr. George Tucker Harrison, which are not the less valuable because they have the note of a charming and absolute unreserve:

" At the university he was one of the most delightful companions, full of life and spirits.   He could sing a good song, and was inimitable as a story-teller.   He endeared himself greatly to his fellow-students, being one of the kindest-hearted of men.   It is needless to say also that, being absolutely natural, and overflowing with good spirits, he was not averse to a little spree, now and then. At the same time, he was a good student, and took the degree of Master of Arts, given only after an undergraduate had passed in all the schools of the university, —ancient languages, modern languages, moral philosphy, natural philosophy, chemistry, and mathematics.   The University of Virginia, founded by Thomas Jefferson, one of the best educated men of his day, and one who was far ahead of his time, was entirely different (at that period) from any other university in this country.   Jefferson brought all the first professors from the Universities of Oxford, Cambridge, and Dublin, in order that the new university should be free from the prejudices of any college then existing in this country.   And it was the first college or university to establish the elective system.

"Dudley was a member of the Delta Kappa Epsilon. He was also a distinguished member of 'The Ugly Club,' a society got up by some of the choice spirits of his time, and to which the principal condition for admission— besides being a good fellow—was abundant homeliness of appearance. It is not said that Dudley, however, ever gained the annual prize,—a pair of boots, given to the member who was voted the 'ugliest' member! It does not seem possible that Bishop Dudley, who, in later life, with his brilliant dark eyes and intellectual, kindly expression, was an attractive figure wherever he went, could have shone in this way in 'The Ugly Club' at the university.

"A love of truth was one of the foundations of his character; and, in addresses to young men, especially, he would always hold up lofty ideals, and urge them never to lower the sacred majesty of truth by resorting to expediency. One of his latest sermons, preached at St. Bartholomew's Church, New York, after the death of his friend and school and college-mate, Virginius Dabney, illustrated this point with great force. He related how Mr. Dabney, being in great financial straits, refused to avail himself of a misunderstanding which would have placed him and his family out of the reach of penury. A certain Civil Service post was open, and Mr. Dabney became an applicant for it. Shortly before this, he had had a slight stroke of apoplexy, which had left him somewhat lame, but had not otherwise impaired his physical or mental health. His testimonials were such as few men have ever, before or since, been able to present;—they were letters from such distinguished men and speaking in such high terms of him. The official in whose hands the appointment lay called on Mr. Dabney, and the arrangements for his receiving the post were practically completed, when, a day or two later, this gentleman met Mr. Dabney out of doors, and said to him : ' I am glad to see that you are sufficiently recovered of your rheumatism, to be able to be out of doors again.' The temptation to let the misapprehension,—which meant bread and butter for himself and family,—pass was very great; but the Virginian said : ' Sir, I am too old now to commence to lie. I am not suffering from rheumatism. I have had a stroke of apoplexy.' The post was, of course, not given to him.

" Bishop Dudley told this story as illustrating the height to which the sense of honour and truthfulness may lead a man. The bishop had a magnificent voice and fine delivery, and was never at a loss for words.

" When he was in England at the Lambeth Conference, in 1897, he was introduced to King Edward, then the Prince of Wales. In conversation, the Prince referred to his visit to the States long ago, and said he had very pleasant reminiscences of his trip to Kentucky. The bishop said he hoped the Prince might be induced to visit them again, to which the Prince said, there was nothing he should like better. ' We boast of superiority in three things in Kentucky,' the bishop went on ; ' we think we have the most beautiful women in America; the finest race-horses; and the best whiskey.'

" During the last twenty years of his life, Bishop Dudley and his wife and children spent every summer with his mother-in-law, Mrs. Aldrich, at Bay Shore, Long Island. He was an enthusiastic fisherman, and delighted to pass the long summer days on the Great South Bay. His devotion to Mrs. Aldrich was one of the sweetest things remembered of him by many. His courteous attentions to her were lover-like, and his attitude towards her certainly refuted the old idea of the relations of a man to his mother-in-law. She trusted him implicitly, and almost her last words, on her deathbed, on hearing that Bishop and Mrs. Dudley had arrived, were, 'What a relief!' And the shock of her death was an indirect cause of his own, two days later in the same house.

"He was an indefatigable worker among his people, and a favourite wherever he went. Perhaps this was due, partly, to his adaptability. Out of his luxurious home in Louisville, he was ready to share, in his visitations, the hospitality of the humble log cabin; and was wont to tell of his experiences on such occasions. Over and over again, he spent the night in a house consisting of but one room, which served as kitchen, parlour, and bedroom. All the members of the family, six or more, passed the night there; but, in order to entertain the bishop with due honour, they hung up a blanket to divide off a part of the room for him to sleep in with some privacy.

"His love of justice was shown in one simple instance —that of a gifted young writer, whose first work was severely attacked by ignorant critics. After months of this persecution, the criticism was effectually silenced by William Dean Howells, then editor of Harper's *Drawer* who, personally unacquainted with the young poet, wrote in the magazine a long article in praise of her work. Bishop Dudley sent Mr. Howells a letter of thanks in behalf of the young author, which only came to the knowledge of her family after her death, through Mr. Howells himself.

'The bishop was not one to care for indiscriminate

praise; but he said once to this same young author:
' My dear, nothing said of me in print ever pleased me
more than those simple words of yours, " The rich flock
to listen to him, and *the common people hear him
gladly.*" ' "

These characteristic recollections of Dr. Harrison's may well be followed by the story of an
incident which the Bishop himself was fond of
recalling, because, like most of his fellow-men,
he enjoyed being commended for his profi-
ciency in a craft which was not his professed
calling.   He was on a hunting expedition near
Louisville, and happened to fall in with a local
sportsman whose unconcealed admiration for
the city man's marksmanship paved the way
for further conversation.

"What's your name?" the countryman
finally inquired.

"Dudley," was the reply.

After some exchange of incident and experience the bishop's interlocutor hazarded:

"Say, Dudley, what business do you follow?"

"I'm a preacher."

"Oh, get out!   What are you giving me?"

"But I am.   I preach every Sunday."

"Where?"

"In Louisville."

"Well, I never! I never would ha' thought it. You ain't stuck up a bit like most of the preachers down this way."

An invitation to hear this new-made acquaintance preach was accompanied by a scribbled card, and the next Lord's Day saw the rustic in his "Sunday best" ushered into the bishop's own pew, where he listened intently to both service and sermon.

He was manifestly amazed, afterward, to have the orator of the morning come down to greet him as cordially and familiarly as in the woods. He managed to stammer his thanks and added:

"I ain't much of a judge of this kind of thing, parson; but I riz with you, and sot with you, and saw the thing through the best I knew how. All the same, if my opinion is worth anything to you, the Lord meant you for a hunter."

It would be interesting to know how much of Bishop Dudley's rare facility in translating himself to "all sorts and conditions of men" came from the training which he received in the army. After his graduation at the University of Virginia, he became a professor of Latin and Greek in the university, and it was there that the Civil War found him. It was

inevitable that he should pass, as did others of
the faculty, and the great mass of the students,
from college walls to the ranks of the army.
In Mr. John Wise's admirable *End of an Era*,
a book which, for its side-lights upon the Civil
War, and for its singular combination of reserve and candour, is one of the most valuable
contributions to American history, is a very
vivid picture of this transformation.   It was inevitable, as I have said, that Dudley should be
influenced by it ; and I apprehend that, to the
end of his episcopate, if he had been asked
what had most helped to make that episcopate
potent for good, he would have named his
army life as among such educative and inspiring powers.   In the schools he learned to
know books : in the army he learned to know
men : and no one who ever saw him dealing
with men could be in any doubt that, wide and
accurate as was his scholarly learning, none of
it could quite have taken the place, or furnished the wisdom, of that large insight and
cool judgment born in camps.

But when the life in camps was ended, he
turned, not unnaturally, to another and a
higher service.   That gravitation toward the
ministry of which Bishop Gibson has lately
spoken, drew him by a supreme attraction to

be the ordained soldier and servant of Jesus
Christ, and the year 1865 saw him a student
in the Theological Seminary of Virginia.

A fellow-student of Dudley's, the beloved
and honoured Bishop of West Virginia, has
favoured me with some seminary recollections
of Dudley, which I transcribe precisely as
written.

"In regard to Bishop Dudley's seminary career, I
make note of certain things that may be of interest.
He was by far the best furnished man that we had, and
we all recognised it, the faculty included. He seems to
have been a special favourite of Dr. Sparrow, who really
taught him a great deal, for his studies had not previously
been along theological lines. On one occasion Dr. Sparrow asked him in class some question regarding the lecture of the day before. In reply, Dudley gave an answer
just the opposite of the doctor's contention. Everybody
was very much surprised, and the good doctor, rapping
his fingers on the arms of his chair, as was his wont,
looked quietly up and said : 'Well, Mr. Dudley, doctors
will differ!'

"While in his senior year, the Rev. Dr. N. H.
Schenck, then rector of Emmanuel, Baltimore, came to
the seminary to try to get Dudley to take charge of his
church during his absence of three or four months. He
had sense enough to decline, but the offer shows the
esteem in which he was held and how his reputation
had gone beyond the seminary walls.

"Our rooms were just opposite, and of course I saw a
great deal of him ;—he delighted in Hooker, and intro-

duced among us *Brown on the Gospels* and Goul-
burn's *Thoughts on Personal Religion.* I have known of
his giving this latter book to several persons;—it was a
great favourite with him.

"He was a great admirer of Dr. Packard. One evening at the doctor's table, when Dudley had been taking
off some one—I think, Dr. Minnegerode—Dr. Packard
said : 'I should not like to think that any one took me
off in that way.' 'Well,' said his wife, 'I have no
doubt but that you are thus taken off as are others.'
'No,' said the doctor, 'that cannot be, because there is
nothing about me they can use in such a way.'

"We used to go to Bishop Johns' a good deal, and the
last week of the session, on missionary evening, we were
there together, and after tea we started on ahead just
enough to open the gate for the bishop, who was going
over to the chapel in his carriage. The old gentleman,
without cracking a smile, flung Dudley a cent, which he
put in his pocket and carried for many a long day.

"We went to 'Sharon'¹ together; and so I heard there
his first expounding. I must say that, beyond the fact
that all the people were devoted to him and admired
him greatly, I have no recollection of his addresses. I
do not think he would care to have had them
published.

"Dudley was very fond of singing, and such exercise
was often carried on in his room, where we all delighted
to congregate. By such gatherings his supremacy was

¹ It was the admirable custom, at the Virginia Seminary, to assign
the students to "Mission Stations," at a convenient distance—vary-
ing from two to five miles—from the seminary, and "Sharon" was
one of these. Here the students conducted services accompanied
by brief addresses. It was at Sharon that Phillips Brooks began his
lay ministry.—H. C. P.

quietly and firmly established, though I am sure that no
one ever saw a more unpretending and genial ruler. He
used to take part in our games—in those days, baseball
—though, owing to his disabled arm, he was somewhat
hindered.

"I don't think any of us were particularly hard
students in those days, though Dudley did wrestle with
Hebrew, and was Dr. Packard's delight in Greek. His
great profit was from Dr. Sparrow,—in public and
private."

It would be easy to infer from these recollections that the late Bishop of Kentucky
was only, or mainly, a kindly, good-natured,
pleasant-mannered person, who took up the
tasks of his great office with an easy-going
and rather superficial view of their nature and
opportunities, and who neither by scholarship
nor episcopal foresight greatly magnified his
calling. But nothing could be more remote
from the fact. Men are by temperament, intellectually, and morally, what they are; and
no one has the moral without the intellectual
temperament that goes with it. Bishop Dudley
had a kindly and sunny disposition, and easy
and unpretentious manners. But, in the highest
sense of that word, he was a scholar;—not a
mass of undigested learning, which dominated
and tyrannised him; but a man to whom exact
knowledge had its legitimate value, and who

was competent, as his companions in the work of preparing the recently authorised version of the Bible with Marginal Readings could testify, to have an opinion upon hermeneutical and exegetical questions based upon adequate study and enquiry.

And so of his character as a ruler and administrator. He had no swift contempt for the men or the traditions that had gone before him; and his tender reverence for the teachers and pastors at whose feet, in his youth, he had sat, was one of the most winning and engaging traits of his maturer years. But he recognised the office of the episcopate as called to be taught supremely by the Holy Ghost, and he realised with a trustful and believing candour that it would often happen that new emergencies in the Church must be met by men and methods adapted to them. He was no Bourbon crying out, for ever, "The past is better!" though the lessons of that past were never absent from his mind.

In a word, he was a man of large vision, and rare intellectual endowments. To whatever task or place he was called in the Church, he rose easily and competently; and when he was chosen chairman of the House of Bishops, which office he held at the time of his death, those who voted for him, some of them, mainly because he was the bishop of a small and central diocese, whose place and claims gave him leisure and contacts which were desirable,— were agreeably surprised to find him illustrate as a presiding officer an ability of the highest order.

But through all these various honours, dignities, and responsibilities, he remained himself —simple, benign, playful, sympathetic, and unspoiled.

It is with such a portraiture of him that I close this sketch. It is from the hand of the Rev. R. Grattan Noland, who knew him intimately, and served under him with unswerving love and loyalty until his removal from the diocese of Kentucky.

"My boyhood was spent in the home of Bishop Dudley's parents-in-law. My first recollection of anything connected with his election is hearing the matter of his election discussed, and receiving the impression that he had accepted the election to be Bishop of Kentucky, partly at least, in fear that otherwise he might be called to be a missionary bishop.

"I now doubt that he could have been more useful anywhere than in Kentucky. For those were somewhat perturbed days for the Church in Kentucky, and another sort of man might easily have emphasised differences existing in that diocese. Oil was surely needed on those troubled waters; and Bishop Dudley had a good

12

deal of oil in the castor. I doubt that he ever left any troubled waters in the wake of his influence.

"Rumour has it that when the young assistant bishop, soon after his consecration, arrived in Kentucky, some one, determined to have 'a line upon' him and his policy, asked him whether he were 'high' or 'low'; to which he replied, 'Sir, I am high, low, Jack, and the game.' I have never been able to discover whether or not this incident really happened; my private opinion is that it just 'growed.' Among a people who (like the Kentuckians) are conversant with 'Jacks' and 'games,' it was very easily possible for such an estimate to be placed upon Bishop Dudley. St. Paul (or even the bishop) might have expressed it otherwise; but the people of Kentucky have ways of their own; and I suspect that they just naturally and instinctively 'sized up' the young bishop (who in large degree was 'all things to all men') in these terms of their own experience. But whether it be considered as the bishop's own declaration of his policy, or as the people's instinctive estimate of him, it was a decided hit. It just covered the ground of his relations, social and ecclesiastical, with the people —all the people.

"He was peculiarly adapted to be 'high, low, Jack, and the game,' with the Kentuckians; and he had, too, a remarkable power of adapting himself. Somehow it just was in him to be *en rapport* with any set of people he came in contact with. With a splendid measure of magnetism, and glowing eloquence, a large fund of humour and anecdote, a wide acquaintance with men and things, a marvellous memory for names and faces, a most charming way of meeting one half-way in entertaining and being entertained, and withal a very sound judg-

ment and large charity, he at once won his way, and
became permanently popular not only within the Church,
but also among all the denominations. If he could not
quite say of the 'Campbellites,' who (like the fish, probably
named after them, the 'new lights') were quite abundant in Kentucky, that they, with him, belonged to the
'army' of the Lord, he could at least say and feel that
they belonged to the 'navy.' It wasn't 'policy' in him
that he got next to all sorts and conditions of men; I
doubt that, strictly speaking, he had much 'policy.' It
was just instinctive, natural—a part of himself. In the
later years of his episcopate, his wider interests in the
larger problems and duties of the Church divorced him
somewhat from this close touch with the common run of
men and women in Kentucky; but up to the very last
the smallest of us felt that it was a delight to be in the
bishop's company—a delight not only because the bishop
was always interesting and entertaining, but also because
he had a way of making us little fellows feel that we, too,
were interesting and entertaining. The fact of the matter is, that, with just half a chance, the bishop loved men
and men loved him.

"I never saw him really self-absorbed, in the dumps,
glum. He was always awake to the environment; he was
always interested in what you were saying, or interesting
you in what he was saying. He had no episcopal shell
into which he withdrew himself—at least not when others
were around. His clergy knew him and enjoyed him;
and he knew and enjoyed them. We never dreaded
him, or sought to get away from him; we always enjoyed
him and wanted to be with him. Once he travelled
some distance with a 'drummer' (as the commercial
traveller was once called). They talked and talked,

each enjoying the other. After a while the drummer asked, 'What house do you represent, sir?' And the bishop replied, 'I represent the House of the Lord; I am the Bishop of Kentucky.' And still they talked on, the drummer somehow feeling that the bishop was a sort of drummer, and the bishop feeling that the drummer was somehow a sort of bishop. He had a knack of making one feel that way. We parsons always had a sort of notion that the bishop was a parson, too.

"His powers of adaptation were marvellous. No man, more than he, liked the best; yet he always managed to get along quite merrily with the worst. When it first fell to my happy lot to have him come to my parish for a visitation, I nearly went broke for a split-box of very good cigars; but he would not touch them; he just wanted a 'stogie' or a pipe, every time. Coming back from the General Convention at San Francisco he was as near to a bad humour as he generally got. He was very tired and 'tuckered out,' and the trip was very mean. He complained of several and varied assortments of maladies, and was in fact greatly in need of coddling and nursing. He had plenty of good cigars, and I tried to tickle his palate with one or two other brands of the best. But it would not go at all; it was always, 'Give me one of those miserable little "stogies" of yours.' I've often wondered if he didn't just want to be comrades with me. Somehow I don't think he could resist that feeling—just to be what the other fellow was, provided the other fellow was clean and true. He was himself singularly clean and true. I do not remember ever to have heard a word of gossip or scandal from his lips. Once or twice he asked me about some rumour that was afloat; but when he found that I had not

heard much about it, and wanted to know the full of it,
he shut up like a clam. I doubt that any parson ever
got from him the tale of another parson's doings.   Yet
barring gossip and lengthy argument—he had no taste for
arguing things—the bishop was ' right in ' any little ' pow-
wow ' we had—as full of news and fun and anecdote as
possible. He would sit by the hour, after service, and
talk and listen so that *we all*, at least, would be sorry when
bedtime came.   I remember a convocation we had up at
Beattyville. Lockwood was then in charge of that mission
and had things booming. Penick, and Ward, and Sneed,
and McCready, and Sheppard, and I—perhaps others—
had jogged over the mountains with the bishop. But,
even after the service that night, none of us—not even
the bishop—seemed tired. We were gathered about a
fire in Lockwood's study, just talking about all sorts of
things in a rambling sort of way, and incidentally smoking. Sneed had the floor, and was telling some yarn
about the Rockies. We were all half listening and half
dozing, when Sneed's hero somehow got mixed up with
a grizzly. In a most innocent way Sneed turned to the
bishop and impressively said, ' And you know, Bishop, a
grizzly is a right dangerous sort of thing.' I think you
could have heard the bishop laugh at a distance of six
blocks. He just doubled up and roared until he cried.
Somehow it is worth so much in a parson's life just to have
a bishop who can laugh that way. It was all a part of
that work that has been going on in Kentucky through-
out his episcopate—this real enjoyment and sense of
comradeship which we all had in the bishop. It helped
to make everything go so smoothly, without discord and
jealousy or the blues. So *he was* ' high, low, Jack, and
the game.'

"But he was more than this. The story is told of an old colored woman, who, having heard very much of the bishop, was anxious to inspect him at close range, and who (upon occasion of one of his visits) had been permitted to serve him with a late breakfast, and particularly cautioned to see to it that he had an abundance of hot cakes. After several rounds of hot cakes, the bishop had fallen, over his breakfast (the breakfast being nearly over), into a brown study. The old lady had some difficulty in attracting his attention to another plate of cakes, and presently, despairing of decorous silence, touched him and asked, 'King Dudley, will you have some cakes?' To many of the 'colored' he was indeed half a king. The bishop had a great fondness for the 'colored folks.' I think it was probably this same old lady who had dubbed him 'king' of whom he once told me. The Methodists were holding a colored revival in the town, and there was much excitement. One of the preachers was a very large man, and the other very small. The bishop met 'Aunt Martha' bustling about the house and asked, 'Well, Aunt Martha, which of your preachers do you like the best—the big, or the little one?' To which Aunt Martha replied, 'Lors, Bishop, I think I likes the little one the bestis; he strain hisself the most.' I think the bishop enjoyed very greatly that estimate of ministerial effectiveness.

"An old colored woman, who had known him long, stood at the station in Louisville awaiting the train which bore his body back home. Her tears were profuse; but even her sorrow was transformed into indignant reproaches, when the train drew in, because they had not draped the engine, as she had heard was done when President McKinley died.

"To others, though he was not a 'king,' he was a *Friend*, writ very large. When his body lay at home in Louisville, there came by night one—a gambler, who had fallen upon the seamy side of life—and asked a daughter's permission to enter. 'He has never passed me on the street, Miss ——,' he said, 'without a Hello ——, a kind shake of the hand, and a God bless you, my boy. I felt that you, Miss ——, would let me come in and see him just once more.' 'T was so; and he, too, wept beside the friend who was gone.

"Many years ago in a little hamlet of the mountains, the bishop stood by the roadside watching a fine horse ridden by. Opposite was a blacksmith shop; and presently there emerged from the smithy a strapping fellow, begrimed and be-aproned, who walked over and said, 'They tell me that you 'se the Bishop of Kaintuckee. I don't know nothin' 'bout what that may be; but I seen you alookin' at that hoss, and I wants to shake.' The bishop shook, and had a chat. He took supper that night with his new friend ; and after a while baptised and confirmed him and his household. Some years later,—I think during a session of the Diocesan Council, —a telegram from the warden of the mission back there in the mountains was handed the bishop. It said that his friend the blacksmith had died the night before, and that his last words were 'tell the bishop that I love him.'

"Up in that mountain village, which he loved, stands a pretty little stone church named 'St. Thomas' in his honour—a monument to one who (variously stated) was bishop,—friend,—king.

"In Bishop Dudley's case the Lord had certainly responded quite generously to that petition of the Litany, which the lay reader got tangled up in—'That it may please thee, to illuminate all bishops, priests, and deacons, so that in due time we may *enjoy them.*'

"I suppose the 'fatted calf' is usually killed for bishops, even though they be not all prodigals. But Bishop Dudley could make a pretty stiff bluff at 'hog and hominy,' if the host had no fatted calf to kill. He enjoyed his meals,—or at least made you think so,—and at table he was himself always enjoyable and an appetiser. He tells the story of a dining-room servant, whose mistress had expressly commanded that hot waffles should be in plenty for the bishop's breakfast. After several innings, there was a pause, and the waiter stood back stiffly from his duties. When nods and winks, in crescendo, failed to bring response, the mistress said, 'John, why do you not hand the bishop some waffles?' 'Huh,' responded John. 'They ain't no mo'; he done had ten already.'

"The bishop's memory for names and faces was notorious. I was standing with him once when a lady, in widow's weeds, walked up and said, 'Of course, Bishop, you do not know me?' He hesitated, I think about two seconds; and then he kissed her, saying, 'Well, don't I though? You were one of my girls in Baltimore twenty years ago, Miss ——.'

"They say that one day he was walking down street with a friend and saw approaching him a man, whom he knew, but whose name had slipped him. He nudged his friend and said, 'Tell me quick, who is this man; his name has utterly gone from me.' Then the man walked up and spoke. Immediately the bishop grasped his hand with a 'How d' ye do, Mr. ——,' and had a little chat, inquiring about various persons and things with which Mr. —— was conversant. After they passed on, the friend inquired, 'How on earth did you get that man's name?' And the bishop confessed that he had seen the initials in his hat when it was doffed. He knew pretty much everybody (who was known) in Kentucky; and not often did a general or a colonel escape him. But upon one occasion some one was telling of Gen. —— of Cynthiana. The bishop could not get the general located. At last he asked, 'Who is this Gen. ——?' The general was described in detail. 'But,' asked the bishop, 'what was he general of? I know that man, but I never heard of his being a general.' And the narrator confessed that he had at one time been general ticket agent of the —— R.R., a rather small railroad, by the way.

"The Bishop of Lexington keeps a list of all the communicants of his diocese, revised from time to time. One day a discussion arose about a Mr. ——, a communicant, at Paris. Bishop Dudley insisted that there was no such 'communicant' at Paris. The Bishop of Lexington got down his book, and lo! there it was in plain black, Mr. ——, a communicant in good standing. But Bishop Dudley still insisted that it was a mistake, and told the story of a Jew, who had 'gotten religion,' *but it was in his wife's name.* We found out later that Mr. —— of Paris was a communicant *in his wife's name.*

"I never knew the bishop to take any liberties with the Prayer Book. On special occasions, of course, he exercised the '*jus liturgicum*'; but on ordinary occasions he stuck to the 'rubrics.' Once he was up in the mountains, and, with the missionary in charge, had had rather a strenuous day of it, winding up, after two services and much gadding about over mountain roads, at —— at 7.30 for evening prayer, sermon, and confirmation. It was in the days of the 'permissive use.' Before going into the chancel, the bishop said, 'Let's have the shortened form to-night.' And —— said, 'How's that, Bishop?' (he was not yet conversant with the 'permissive use'). The bishop explained that after the 'opening sentences' we were permitted to say, 'Let us humbly confess our sins unto Almighty God,' etc. After the 'Processional,' —— read, 'The Lord is in His holy temple; let all the earth keep silence before Him,' and then (as though he had just discovered a 'mare's nest') turned to the congregation and with a voice full of exultation said, 'We are permitted to say, let us humbly confess our sins unto Almighty God.' The bishop was immensely refreshed!

"The bishop was not much of a hand at 'butting into' things to settle them by his episcopal authority. In one of my parishes quite a disturbance had been brewed over a new organ. It waxed warmer and warmer, until I thought it would get the better of me. But the bishop never said a word, until the occasion of his visitation. After the services that night, the congregation gathered about him in the body of the church, and some one pointed out the new organ as the bone of contention. The bishop turned and looked at the organ and exclaimed, 'What! that little box of whistles!' And the organ question was settled.

"In another one of my parishes, we had a 'row' with a mission started by the parish, and now—desirous of becoming independent—on the property of, and so much per year from, the parish. There was much correspondence between the mission and parish, and

things were getting ugly. At last the mission appealed
to the bishop, and the bishop gave me quite a scolding,
—a sort of curtain lecture. I had an overweening
anxiety to give the other fellows rope, so I didn't say
very much. The bishop did not officially interfere,
though the affair was considerably aired in the papers;
only now and then he would give it to me privately. At
last I got tired of it, and made a copy of all the correspondence, duly certified before a notary; and went
down to visit the bishop. When he got me by myself
he began on me again. I asked, 'Why do you not come
up and investigate this matter officially?' 'Because,
sir,' he said, 'that would bring the fuss officially before
the public, and I want none of that. But you can settle
this matter yourself, and why do you continue to permit
that little mission to be dealt with so ungenerously?' I
handed him the certified copy of the correspondence and
asked him to read it. After reading he got up and,
looking straight at me, said, '——, somebody has lied;
and I thank God it isn't you.' He didn't take the matter up officially, but somehow the 'row' quieted down
at once.

"There were two parsons in his diocese whom he
had a special right, perhaps, to scold. One night, after
some function in the house, we, bed-fellows on the third
floor, entered into a collusion to have it out with his
'lordship' the next morning. We were just tired of
being treated as though we were still 'kids,' and were determined that, before another day passed, he should
understand that we were men and priests. Somehow
the next morning we were so enamoured of being 'still
kids' with the bishop, that we just forgot to remind him
that we were men and priests;—the fact is that he half

made us feel that we were members of the House of Bishops. He had that way, somehow. I 've known of several persons who were 'miffed' at the bishop, and got over it without an apology from him ; and I have never known a single person, who really knew him, who stayed 'miffed' at anything that he happened to do.

"While he was at the General Convention in San Francisco, the Louisville papers somehow conceived the idea that he was to be elected Bishop of Long Island, and debated the question of his removal to Brooklyn. Coming back on the train, I asked him if there were any truth in the report; and if he had been 'sounded' upon the matter. I found him rather interested, though he seemed to have no 'tip' on the whole subject. If the rumour were true, he seemed to be inclined to consider it. He explained to me that he was getting too old for such a diocese as Kentucky, and might be of more use in a more compact diocese; but his chief interest, I gathered, lay in a test of the question of the transfer of a diocesan bishop. He thought that, at his age, and being chairman of the House of Bishops, he might put that question to the test with dignity. I doubt, however, that he would have done anything more than merely feel the pulse of the House of Bishops in regard to the transfer, or that he would seriously have considered leaving Kentucky.

" The bishop was never much of a stickler for points. I know of no instance of his endeavouring to carry his own way by storm. He would state his views, or desires, or requests; and bolster them up with his usually well-considered reasons; but, after that, he would let the other side have its say, and then he would rest his case. It sometimes seemed to me that he was over-scrupulous

and over-sensitive about being perfectly square in push-
ing any enterprise. I've never known him in the least
degree to descend to wire-pulling. It was, I think, by
no means his real choice that the diocese should be
divided. In the Diocesan Council of 1895 he proposed
in his address the election of a bishop coadjutor, and
offered to relinquish a portion of his salary to make the
plan feasible. The matter was regularly and thoroughly
discussed. During the discussion, one of the clergy, ap-
pealing for this relief to the bishop, declared, in a fine
burst of eloquence, that it was but just to our 'beloved
bishop, who with such untiring diligence and faithfulness
has ministered to us now these 1900 years' (it was the
bishop's 19th anniversary). This, of course, brought
down the house. But nothing could easily bring down
—— when he got on his high horse of eloquence; and,
after a puzzled pause, he repeated himself in the identical words a little more impressively. We adjourned
for luncheon after that.

"But the 'resolution' was carried; and the standing
committee was instructed to ask consent to the election
of a bishop coadjutor. After the council had adjourned,
there arose some dispute concerning the methods used
in carrying the resolution, and there was talk of 'sharp
practice.' I doubt that even the silliest talker suspected
for a moment that the bishop had any finger in this supposed 'sharp practice.' But the mere word hurt the
bishop; and he at once 'withdrew his consent.' The
project was then started for a division of the diocese.
After some time, filled with gathering of statistics and
interviews, a plan was perfected for 'division,' which
was to be discussed at a meeting of the Lexington convocation, which was practically coterminous with the

present diocese of Lexington. I was assured that the
bishop had been interviewed, and that his consent
could be had to this project, if it could be carried
through the council; in fact, I was assured that the
bishop '*wanted*' this. But, despite all assurances, I had
an idea that 'division' was very decidedly the bishop's
second choice, and that he only 'wanted' it if the other
alternative, 'the coadjutor,' was out of the question. On
my way to the convocation, I took occasion to spend the
night at the bishop's, where some of my relatives were
staying. I discovered that the bishop had, in interviews
with several of the clergy of the Lexington convocation,
expressed a willingness to have the proposed plan of
division put to the test, promising his canonical consent
if the plan proved feasible. Then I pulled out of my
pocket a paper, which I had prepared, the gist of which
was a 'resolution' calling upon the standing committee
to execute the order of the council in the matter of the
coadjutor, and told the bishop that I, proposed to offer
that at the meeting of the convocation. Immediately
he turned on me pretty sharply and said, '——, don't
you know, sir, that I have *withdrawn my consent* to the
election of a bishop coadjutor?' In reply I stated the
facts: he had formally come before the council with a
proposal—almost a request—for the election of a coadjutor ; he had formally given his canonical consent ; the
council had formally acted and formally instructed the
standing committee to execute its desire in the matter.
'Is this a matter,' I asked, 'which is any longer in your
hands ? Can you, after this action, withdraw your consent ?' I may be mistaken : it is sometimes difficult to
judge men by their faces ; but the bishop had a rather
expressive face ; and I think I read there a feeling of

relief,—a feeling as of one who saw a way out. At any rate, the bishop said, '——, you are right ; I have acted *ultra vires ;* I shall so notify the standing committee.' Then I sat there in the bishop's study, and re-wrote, at his dictation, the preamble and resolution, which the next day I gave notice to the convocation I would present on the following morning.

"The bishop was to go to the convocation. But I did n't want to seem to be in collusion with him in this matter—indeed I was n't ; I had evolved this whole brilliant scheme out of my own head ; and I and my parish were more radically opposed to 'division' than the bishop. But when a youngster happens once in a while to do what he thinks is a smart thing, he is apt to lay it on pretty thick ; and I just then grew 'wondrous wise.' The bishop had a slight cold. In the house was the bishop's father-in-law, my uncle, a doctor. I went off to the doctor's room, and laid the whole scheme I had hatched before him. The upshot of it was that a telegram was sent to the Lexington convocation saying that the doctor forbade the bishop to leave his house for a day or two. Alas! had the bishop been there, another story might have been told. I gave notice that I had a resolution of some importance which I would present the following morning; and as I did n't want to take snap-judgment upon the convocation, I would place it in the hands of the secretary, and ask the privilege of bringing it up, and making some explanatory remarks upon it at 10 o'clock in the morning. When the morning came I arose to call up my 'resolution,' and began my remarks, when lo ! a brother arose and moved to lay the 'resolution' on the table, declaring that he personally had interviewed the bishop and that the bishop 'wanted' the other thing; so also said several others. I begged for just a word of explanation, but was 'rapped' down and cried down. In sitting down I managed to yell out, 'The bishop wants this,' which cost me for several months the friendship of three parsons. My resolution—even unread and unexplained —was tabled and I was sat on harder than at any other time in my life. Ah! had the bishop only *not* had a cold! The diocese was practically divided that day in the Lexington convocation,—and, poor me, I was not even permitted to 'peep.' Once before, I believe, an ass opened his mouth; and the Lord's way prevailed!"

Archbishop Tait   Archbishop Benson

Archbishop Temple

Archbishop Tait. Archbishop Benson Archbishop Temple

RECOLLECTIONS OF THREE ARCHBISHOPS

THIS volume was undertaken, as its preface indicates, to recall a few American bishops, chiefly identified with the history of the middle of the nineteenth century; and nothing would at first view seem more remote from its purpose than a retrospect which crossed the Atlantic.

But, in truth, that retrospect would be signally incomplete if it did not recognise the paternal and increasingly felicitous relation which, during the period that I have designated, grew into benign and affectionate existence between British and American prelates.

"Grew," I have said, and that word describes, with sufficient exactness, precisely what came to pass. It cannot be pretended that, in

the beginning, there was, on the one side or
the other, any very keen or tender interest.
The succession of bishops in the United States
came, originally, from two sources, one of them
Scottish, and the other Anglican. The United
States of the present were originally British
colonies ; and when those colonies broke the
tie that had originally bound them to their
mother, the ecclesiastics of the mother Church
did not feel any especial tenderness toward
"wayward children," and the "wayward children" were, in the new United States, like the
early Christians, a "despised sect, everywhere
spoken against."

When, therefore, it became evident that, if
the Church in America was to survive, it must
have bishops of its own, an effort was made to
obtain them from England. But the Church
in England was established,—fast bound to
the State by many and intimate ties ; and the
problem, in London, of giving consecration to
American bishops whose civil obligations constrained them to disown the authority of the
British Crown, was not an easy one. I may
not here rehearse the story of their Anglican
failures ; but it was not unnatural that these
should have led Churchmen in Connecticut to
turn to their Scottish brethren, who, like their

brethren in America, had become dissevered from the State, and yet had conserved the primitive and Apostolic order, doctrine, and worship of the Church of England.

To this end, a convention of the clergy and laity in what is now the Diocese of Connecticut, in the year 1784, chose Dr. Samuel Seabury to be consecrated bishop, and sent him, for that purpose, with appropriate and sufficient testimonials, to Aberdeen. Dr. Seabury was duly consecrated by the *Primus* of Scotland, the Bishop of Aberdeen (Kilgour); his coadjutor (Skinner); and the Bishop of Moray and Ross (Petrie), in the Bishop's Chapel at Aberdeen; and, after signing a *concordat* with the Church of Scotland, affirming the agreement of his own branch of the Church in doctrine, discipline, and worship with that of the Church in Scotland, speedily returned to his work.

Meantime, as I have said, Churchmen elsewhere in the United States were endeavouring to obtain the consecration of their bishops from the See of Canterbury; but the difficulties were grave and the delays unavoidable; and it was not until the year 1787 that the first Bishop of New York (Provoost), and the first Bishop of Pennsylvania (White), were consecrated, on Sunday, February 4th, in Lambeth Chapel by the Archbishop of Canterbury (Moore) ; the Archbishop of York (Markham) ; the Bishop of Bath and Wells (Moss), and the Bishop of Peterborough (Hinchcliffe). Later, Bishop Provoost, of New York, assisted by Bishop Seabury, of Connecticut, and Bishop White, of Pennsylvania, consecrated Bishop Claggett, of Maryland, thus uniting both lines—English and Scotch—in the American succession, which has descended in unbroken stream to the present time.

But not, as has been intimated, with any special transatlantic enthusiasm in either direction. Our American experiment did not greatly interest, and could not consistently attract Churchmen who were either Establishmentarians or Monarchists—or both ; and the American temper, sensitive to criticism, somewhat inflated with the boundless self-confidence of youth, and cold toward a mother the generosity of whose earlier beneficence was easily forgotten when that beneficence was followed by the silence of disapproval, or the coldness of unspoken distrust,—hardened into a chronic reserve.

Such, it must honestly be owned, was the

situation until the year 1868; for, while there had been in personal instances a cordial welcome in Great Britain for individual American bishops, whose brilliant gifts and loving enthusiasm for their Anglican mother won for them a very warm place in Anglican hearts and homes, it cannot be denied that the great majority of American Churchmen regarded that mother with avowed dislike, or concealed suspicion.

It was given to a Canadian bishop—unless I have been misinformed—to bring this infelicitous state of things to an end. There are others to whom that honour has been ascribed; and it is not at all impossible that a great thought—for it was a great thought—had been seething in the mind of more than one cisatlantic bishop, when Bishop Lewis, of Ontario, later Archbishop of Canada, suggested to the then Archbishop of Canterbury, the Most Reverend Dr. Longley, that he should invite the bishops of the Anglican communion in both hemispheres to meet at Lambeth. They did so in the summer of 1868; and every *1867* ten years thereafter (except in 1897, when the conference was arranged for that year to coincide with Queen Victoria's Diamond Jubilee) the Lambeth Conference has been held.

When it sat in 1878, I was not a member of the House of Bishops; and my knowledge of the Conference was merely accidental, but it brought me into contact with the Archbishop of Canterbury, the Most Reverend Archibald Campbell Tait, of whom, in these recollections it will be my privilege first of all to speak.

I

THE MOST REVEREND DR. ARCHIBALD CAMPBELL TAIT, ARCHBISHOP OF CANTERBURY FROM 1868 TO 1882

Archibald Campbell Tait—of Scottish parentage, as his name very clearly indicates—was born at Edinburgh on December 22, 1811. His school life was mainly passed in Edinburgh; and it ought to interest Americans that one of the poems for which, as a pupil in the Edinburgh Academy, he won a prize, was a set of Latin hexameters on "American Independence." The boy grew up side by side with a young kinsman whose parents were Church-people; and when, later, he won what was known as the "Snell Exhibition," and went, on that "Foundation," to Oxford, he became an undergraduate of the University in Balliol College. It was while at

The Most Reverend
Doctor Archibald Campbell Tait,
Archbishop of Canterbury.
From a photograph reproduced by permission of
Elliott & Fry, London.

Oxford that he was confirmed by the Bishop
of Oxford, of that time, and a little later won a
scholarship in Balliol itself.   On Trinity Sunday, 1836, he was ordained deacon by Dr.
Richard Bagot, Bishop of Oxford, and soon
after became curate of March Baldon, in a
desolate region some five miles from Oxford.
Years afterward when, as Bishop of London,
he instituted there some novel and unconven-
tional places for mission work among the poor,
he recalled the lessons he had learned, as a
stripling, in March Baldon.

Tait remained a tutor in Oxford until, in
1842, he was chosen to succeed Dr. Thomas
Arnold as Head Master of Rugby School.   At
Rugby he spent seven years, and was then appointed Dean of Carlisle.   The Rugby life
was an anxious and laborious one, and the
trepidation with which his friends contemplated
his attempting it is curiously illustrated by a
letter from one of the most intimate of them,
Arthur Penrhyn Stanley, afterwards Dean of
Westminster, which began, " My dear Tait, the
awful intelligence of your election has just
reached me."   In other words, men who had
known and worshipped Arnold as Stanley had,
looked with dismay upon the audacity of any
one who should undertake to succeed him.

Tait, however, not only made the venture, but,
though he could never rival Arnold, illustrated
in his work at Rugby some of the noblest
traits and aptitudes of his rare character.
Broken in health, and overwhelmed by tasks
that were too great for any man, he turned
gratefully, when the call came to him, to what
he and his friends supposed, at the time, would
afford to him for the rest of his life the dignified repose of an English deanery. But it soon
became evident to the people of Carlisle that
it was to be no merely dignified repose to him.
In the cathedral, and out of it, among all
classes and ages, he made himself a helpful
and inspiring power; and when, in 1856, he was
called to be Bishop of London, he took with
him to that larger sphere, not alone a store of
experiences, but of developed powers, which
made him ideally fit for the tremendous tasks of
that see. It is a familiar tradition that to that
lofty place in the life of the Church of England
he was called by the choice of the Queen ; and
that Victoria's mother-heart had been drawn to
him by the exceptional bereavement which,
through a visitation of scarlet-fever, had taken
from him in a month five daughters. I have
no smallest doubt that that sorrow won from
his sovereign the tenderest sympathy ; but I

have as little that she was abundantly certified of his great gifts, and his rare character, by testimony as august as it was competent.

Never, indeed, in the history of the Church of England was there an appointment to the see of London more felicitous and fit. It was an hour of transitions,—of awakenings,—of large and novel emergencies. And, step by step, Tait rose to every one of them with steadily greatening grasp and discernment.

This is not the place to rehearse the evidence of this as it was presented, *e. g.*, in his masterly dealings with *Essays and Reviews*, and with the case of Bishop Colenso. The former was the case of a volume of papers of very unequal merit which antagonised the opinions of the great majority of Anglican Churchmen. The latter raised questions, both dogmatic and political, which involved not only a traditional view of the Bible, widely held, but also the matter of the relation of Colonial sees to their Anglican mother, and the competency of Colonial metropolitans to erect their own opinions into absolute standards of the Church's discipline. Looking back upon the whole dreary business, now, with the fuller light of a later scholarship, and with a more truly catholic interpretation of the Church's standards, there is something sublime in the quiet firmness with which the Bishop of London defined and maintained his ground. Arrayed against him were the great majority of the bishops of the hour ; and foremost among these were men who, like Samuel Wilberforce, then of Oxford, had the popular ear as the champions of orthodoxy. But neither their fierce and denunciatory words, nor those of the Bishop of Capetown, moved Bishop Tait in the smallest degree. He did not either admire or agree with Bishop Colenso, or with most of the authors of *Essays and Reviews.* But he knew the law of the Church, and the just limits in it of freedom of speech ; and no theological hysterics, however violent or abusive, could avail to disturb or constrain him. He stood his ground, and in due time, the best minds in the Church owned that he was right.

Bishop Tait became Archbishop of Canterbury in 1868, and it was as such that I first knew him. His son Craufurd, then in orders, visited the United States in the year 1877, and charmed us all by a quality which at that time, at any rate, was rare in his countrymen. Most Englishmen, however laboriously they strove to conceal it, could not quite hide their surprise, and, oftener than

otherwise, their disapproval, of customs different from their own. They resented it that an
American would not say "different *to*"; and it
was quite in vain that one showed them the
passage in the fifteenth chapter of St. Paul's
first Epistle to the Corinthians, in which, in
the English Bible and in King James's version, it is said that "One star differeth *from*
another star in glory" (v. 41). The Bible
might say what it pleased; but English
custom said thus and so, and that settled the
question. The average English traveller could
not see that what exasperated the American
was the assumption that English usage settled
any question,—that it was not further debat-
able,—and that whatever other men or nations
might say was a matter of profound indifference.
The charm of the Reverend Craufurd Tait
consisted in the fact that, among other graces,
he had a singularly open mind ; and, while he
did not conceal his surprise, or dissent from,
what was unfamiliar, he had a scholar's curiosity concerning much that must needs have
jarred upon his wonted traditions, or modes of
usage. He had a surprising aptitude for
entering into situations that were mentally, as
well as otherwise, unfamiliar to him ; and he
had a genius of swift appreciation for things

which were the product of the needs of our
Western civilisation, and which Anglican conservatism had been wont to regard with reserve
or suspicion, which, to his American hosts, was
a perpetual delight. I was at that time a New
York rector, and he was for a time our guest
at the rectory. It was my privilege, as secretary of the House of Bishops, to introduce him
to that body when, during the General Convention of 1877, the Presiding Bishop invited
him to address the House. The convention
sat in Boston, and everybody in that somewhat undemonstrative community was as
swiftly won by him as we had been in New
York. He made a brief address in each of the
two Houses of the convention, attracting all
hearts by his singular modesty and evident
culture ; and returned, soon afterwards, to
England. He had not been long at home
before he fell ill, and in a few months was no
more.

As it happened, I was in London in the
spring of 1878 with two of my children. I did
not intrude upon the Archbishop of Canterbury ; first, because of his recent and sore
affliction, and, second, because the Lambeth
Conference was then about to assemble, and
Lambeth Palace was besieged by bishops, of

whom I was not then one. But the archbishop
found me out in my modest little London
hotel, and insisted that my children and I
should come and stay at Lambeth. I shall
never forget the morning of our arrival there.
My children were shown at once to their room,
and I was conducted to the archbishop's
study. It is now nearly thirty years since I
then, for the first time, saw him ; but I remember the whole incident as though it had
happened yesterday. After a few exchanges of
greeting and enquiry of the usual sort, he said,
"You knew Craufurd ?   He stayed under your
roof ?" and then rising, he walked to a desk,
nearby, and took from it a photograph of his
son. Handing it to me he said, " Does that
look like him ?" and as I stood looking at the
bright young features, he turned his back to
me, covered his face with his hands, and burst
into tears.

I have never seen emotion which so deeply
moved me. Archbishop Tait had that about
him that recalled his own Scotch granite.
And to see that stately figure and self-
contained prelate swept off his feet, as it were,
by the strong tide of parental feeling, was a
sight never to be forgotten.

One other incident I recall of that charming

visit, which was equally individual and characteristic. We had come to Sunday, and I had
been preaching in the morning, for a London
divine of some eminence and of numerous doctrinal eccentricities. At the lunch-table, Mrs.
Tait, the type of whose Churchmanship was
much more accentuated than her husband's,
said, from her end of the table, " Dr. Potter,
where have you been this morning?" " I have
been preaching for Mr. H——," I answered.
" Preaching for Mr. H——!" she screamed.
And then, calling out to the archbishop she
added, " My dear, do you know where Dr.
Potter has been this morning? He has been
preaching for Mr. H——!" " Well," said the
archbishop, " I am glad of it. I hope he
preached the Gospel!" (which, it was generally believed, was not often heard in Mr.
H——'s pulpit), and the incident was closed.

It was a fine and characteristic illustration of
a really great nature. The archbishop probably
liked Mr. H——, and his theological vagaries,
as little as his wife liked them. But he never
dignified such vagaries by attacking them;
and he realised that American curiosity concerning this or any other ecclesiastical oddity
would be less vigorously stimulated by silence
than by criticism.

Archbishop Tait has been called a great statesman rather than a great ecclesiastic. He was, in fact, a great ecclesiastical statesman; and one shudders to think what might have befallen the Church in Great Britain if, in that eventful era through which he lived, he had not been given to it.

II

THE MOST REVEREND DR. EDWARD WHITE

BENSON, ARCHBISHOP OF CANTERBURY

FROM 1882 TO 1896

On a morning early in 1884 I had an errand which took me to the designer's room in a great establishment in New York, the reputation of which for artistic taste is world-wide. At the moment, the gentleman whom I had called to see was absent; but on his desk there stood a sketch, made with rare skill, which at once caught my eye. It represented a lad clad in an Eton cap and jacket, with light flowing hair, holding a book under his arm, and running. Underneath the picture was written, "The Archbishop of Canterbury, as I remember him." Presently there entered the artist for whom I was waiting, and pointing to the picture, I said:

"What does that mean?"

"Just what it says," was his answer. "Edward White Benson, who has just been made Archbishop of Canterbury, and I were schoolfellows, at King Edward's School (the head master of which was then the famous Prince Lee, afterwards Bishop of Manchester), in Birmingham. Benson's father was a chemist, and also an inventor and author, with a rare enthusiasm for botany. The figure that I have sketched on yonder card" (it will be found on p. 27 of Archbishop Benson's Life by his son, but without any acknowledgment of its source) "was a very familiar one in my boyhood. Benson's way to King Edward's School lay past our door; and often, when I knew that *I* should be late to school, I looked out of the window and saw 'White Benson,' as we were wont to call him, running thither that he might not be."

The boy who was a pupil in King Edward's School in Birmingham went thence, as a sizer, to Cambridge University, was graduated there with honour, and soon afterwards was chosen to be a master at Rugby School. He illustrated here the qualities that subsequently on broader fields found striking opportunity; and it was not surprising that when Wellington College was

The Most Reverend
Doctor Edward White Benson,
Archbishop of Canterbury

From a photograph reproduced by permission of
Elliott & Fry, London.

The Most Reverend
Doctor Edward White Benson,
Archbishop of Canterbury.

founded for the education of the sons of military men, and as a memorial of the great Duke of Wellington, he was called to be its first head master.   Some fifteen years of a schoolmaster's anxious work led him to crave the repose of a less arduous life; and in 1872, though at large pecuniary sacrifice, he accepted from Bishop Christopher Wordsworth of Lincoln an invitation to be the chancellor of the diocese, with the additional rank of canon in the cathedral.   He made his position one of various service and influence, and revealed powers which, when, in 1876, the diocese of Truro was created out of Exeter, led Lord Beaconsfield to offer him that see.   He served it with rare enthusiasm, and with brilliant results; and when, in 1882, Canterbury became vacant, it would not be an exaggeration to say that the best elements in the Church of England turned to him, and hailed with wide thanksgiving his nomination by Mr. Gladstone to the primacy.

I came to know him six years later when the Lambeth Conference of 1888 was convened, in July, in the library of Lambeth Palace.   He was an admirable presiding officer, and a matchless host;—in the latter respect, I think, altogether exceptional.   Our

English brethren illustrate their insularity of
character in nothing more amusingly than in
their bland assumption that the social usages,
hours, etc., of the British Isles are those of
the whole round world,—known and read of
all men, and never, by any chance, to be stated
or explained, but always and everywhere to be
taken for granted. A venerable American
bishop from one of our Western States is said
to have visited England, long before the days
of Archbishop Benson, and to have been
asked by the Archbishop of Canterbury of that
time to be a guest at Lambeth Palace. The
bishop and his wife arrived late in the afternoon, just as the household was assembling in
the drawing-room for "afternoon tea." In
this they were bidden to join ; and albeit
rather discouraged by the scanty nature of the
repast,—for they had made a long day's jour-
ney and had had nothing since a very early
breakfast,—they ate as freely as they were permitted of everything in sight. Then the
mistress of the house rose and, without further explanation, said, "The servant will show
you to your rooms." The bishop and his
wife were somewhat staggered, for in that
Western home from which they came, tea
or "supper" was a much heartier and some-

what later meal; and, after it, people did not immediately retire; but the air of the hostess was somewhat mandatory; and they meekly followed the servant to their rooms. There they sat, in one of the windows looking out upon the somewhat dreary vision of smut and chimney pots which so widely saluted them, until at length the bishop, looking at his watch, said, "Well, my dear, I am very tired, and I think I will go to bed." Proceeding with some deliberation to do so, the episcopal person had just comfortably tucked itself between the sheets, when there came a sharp rap at the door. "Yes," said the bishop, who was already dozing, "what is it?" Answered the voice of the butler from without, "It is half-past eight, my lord, and *dinner* will be on the table in five minutes!"

Such a thing could not have happened in Archbishop Benson's time. He recognised, with a swift intuition, that the habits of foreigners, and the habits of Britons might not be identical; and his household was ordered upon a wise forethought, with abundant information for every guest. Of course, it illustrated Anglican customs; but if there were others, he did not resent them as barbaric intrusions. I remember an evening at Lambeth, when I had the privilege of being his guest there, which illustrates this. It was during the Lambeth Conference, and when the palace was full of guests. The dinner had been large, long, and —I wonder if I may dare to add—dull; and we were gathered in the drawing-room in that ante-climax of the evening which no one who has experienced it can very joyfully remember. At that moment the present Archbishop of Canterbury, who was then the Dean of Windsor, and one of the secretaries of the Lambeth Conference, rose and said, in a voice intended to be heard by the whole company, "Well, I fear I must go to my work"; and then, *sotto voce*, as he passed my chair, "If you care to come to my room, I will give you a cigar." It should be noted, here, that, at that time, the hearts of our British brethren had not greatly softened to American infirmities; and smoking, in an episcopal palace, was regarded as somewhat profane. But I fear that I followed the Dean of Windsor with unseemly eagerness; and, for an hour or more, "burnt incense unto Baal," as a good old American bishop used to describe it, with keen delight. It was long after midnight when I took leave of the dean, and set out for my room. My cigar was still in my hand, and my way lay through a long, dark hall, at the other end of which were the staircase and the archbishop's study. I had nearly reached the former when, to my horror, the door of the study was opened, and his grace stood revealed in the bright light which streamed through it. There was nothing to be said, and no avenue for retreat. Covered with dismay, and with the witness of my guilt in my fingers, I stood transfixed. But in a moment there came the archbishop's bubbling "Ha! Ha! New York! I have caught you, red-handed!" and then, as he passed on, that kindly twinkle of his eye, and that radiant and luminous smile which no one who ever saw them will forget!

Indeed, it was this genius of humour, and the singular felicity of its expression, which were among Archbishop Benson's most exquisite gifts. He was remarkable for the exceptional facility with which he used his rare mastery of the classics in this connection; and his genius in casting his phrases into some form of medieval Latin was something which I have never seen matched. But, whether Latin or English, it did not matter. His rare charm lay in that swift facility with which, very often, he redeemed an embarrassing moment by some playful term which took all the sting out of acrimonious words, or an awkward situation. At the Lambeth Conference, one of the topics was " Socialism " ; and one of the speakers enlarged upon the vices of modern society with a good deal of heat ; dwelling, I remember, with especial bitterness upon what he called the "irritating indulgence of display, by the rich, as illustrated particularly by their 'liveried menials.' " The phrase seemed to me, as I caught it, somewhat infelicitous ; and I found myself recalling the archbishop's servants in their sober liveries, and thinking, in view of their courteous guidance, and our frequent appeals to them for that guidance—which we should hardly have ventured to make if we had not been enabled, by their dress, to identify them—I found myself thinking, I say, that the philippic concerning " liveried menials " might wisely have been omitted, or that, at any rate, such acrid criticism of a usage followed by our gracious host might wisely have been postponed.

It was while my mind was occupied with these reflections that the paper was concluded, and the speaker sat down. The essay had been able, and the subject was profoundly interesting. But the pause that followed its conclusion was considerable, and the situation was awkward.

In a moment, however, the silence was broken by the voice of the archbishop, as he drew his watch from his pocket, and having consulted it, turned toward us a most genial face : " It is now twenty minutes after one," he said, " and luncheon is to be served in ten minutes.   No adequate discussion of the admirable paper to which we have just listened could be had in ten minutes; and it will be well to postpone it until after the mid-day recess.   I will, therefore, declare the conference adjourned for that purpose ; and now, brethren," added the archbishop with that charming twinkle in his eye, "the 'liveried menials' will show you the way to the dining-room."   There went up, straightway, a shout of laughter from the conference, and, in parliamentary phrase, "the incident was closed."

Alas that the reign in Lambeth of that charming personality was so soon to be ended ! I need not rehearse, here, the dramatic and pathetic conclusion of that gifted life.   But no one who knew it will ever forget it, and no American guest at Lambeth who enjoyed that beaming hospitality will be unmindful of the charming and noble manhood that enshrined it !

III.

THE MOST REVEREND DR. FREDERICK TEMPLE,
ARCHBISHOP OF CANTERBURY, FROM 1896 TO 1902

Dr. Frederick Temple, at that time head master of Rugby School, where he had gone in succession to Dr. Archibald Campbell Tait, when the latter became Dean of Carlisle, first came into general notice in connection with the volume once famous under the title of *Essays and Reviews*. Dr. Temple's essay was entitled "The Education of the World," and propounded a view of the Bible and of God's dealings with the people of Israel which is now, I suppose, universally accepted. Forty years ago, however, it was not only unfamiliar, but, as many devout people honestly believed, heterodox ; and the volume in which it appeared had other essays which even the most advanced scholars regarded with apprehension, if not with positive disfavour.

When, therefore, Dr. Temple was nominated for the see of Exeter, especially as it was in succession to a bishop (Philpotts) of most aggressive conservatism, there was a fierce outcry of dissent from all quarters of the Church ; and even a menace of resistance to his confirm-

The Most Reverend Doctor Frederick Temple,
Archbishop of Canterbury.
From a photograph reproduced by permission of the
London Stereoscopic Society.

ation in Bow Church, which provoked general alarm.

But Dr. Temple made a good Bishop of Exeter; and, when Tait was promoted from London to the primacy, was obviously the fittest man to succeed him. When I came to know him, Benson was Archbishop of Canterbury, and Temple his suffragan in the see of London; but it was obvious enough that Benson had not forgotten the days when he was a master at Rugby, and Temple, as head master, had been his chief. Indeed, I do not recall anything more charming than the affectionate deference of the archbishop to his venerable junior. It was in every way appropriate, therefore, that when Benson was so suddenly cut off, Temple should succeed him; and it was as Archbishop of Canterbury, in 1897, that I first came to know him intimately. I had been in Southern Europe during that winter, and the Archbishop of Canterbury, learning that I was to be in England some weeks before the date at which the Lambeth Conference was appointed, did me the honour to ask me to attend a meeting of the committee of arrangements for that conference which he had called at the "Church House."

The "Church House" was a structure

erected in Dean's Yard, Westminster, under
the auspices of Archbishop Benson; and it tard-
ily supplied for the Church what had long
been needed in London. Here Archbishop
Temple had summoned the Archbishops of
York and Dublin, the *Primus* of the Church in
Scotland, and the Bishops of Winchester, Durham, and others, to meet him, and confer as to
the arrangements for the approaching Lambeth
Conference. He had hardly taken his seat,
however, before the Bishop of Durham (Dr.
Westcott) rose in his place, and with a face
flushed with emotion, read from a paper that
he held in his shaking hand, some outlines of
the arrangements, prepared by the Archbishop
of Canterbury himself. These arrangements
contemplated that the conference should hold
some of its sessions in the Church House rather
than in the library of Lambeth Palace, which
latter was but poorly suited for a deliberative
body, and sure to be much overcrowded.

It was upon this proposal that the Bishop of
Durham fastened with, what seemed to me,
needlessly vehement emotion. He described
the plan of holding some of the sessions of the
conference elsewhere than in Lambeth as sure
to cause many of the bishops unmixed grief.
He described it as the menace of changes still

more radical, yet to come; and concluded by saying, "Most Reverend Sir, at this rate, I should not be surprised to hear it proposed, before we adjourn, that the next Lambeth Conference shall be held in *New York!*"

The Bishop of Durham sat down, and the Bishop of Manchester (Morehouse) controlled his mirth sufficiently to say, "The Bishop of New York is present; and I am sure he will assure the Bishop of Durham of the great pleasure that it would give our American friends to welcome the Lambeth Conference."

The Bishop of Durham, who, until that moment, had been quite unaware of my presence, turned to me with a most rueful countenance, and made his apologies; and, as I need hardly say, I eagerly rose to assure the committee that the Bishop of Durham's idea was not new to us in America, and would be enthusiastically received on our side of the Atlantic.

But what, most of all, impressed me in this somewhat amusing as well as awkward scene, was the absolute silence of the archbishop. He bent his head and covered his face with his hands while his brother of Durham denounced the archiepiscopal proposals; but he said nothing to stay the storm of disapproval with which his plans had been visited, save that, when the committee adjourned, and we scattered, he turned to me and said, "Come over to Lambeth to dinner!" I did so; and though for some hours he made no further allusion to the subject, he turned to me at the dinner-table and said, "How would this room do for the conference?" We were dining in the noble "state dining-room," an apartment quite vast enough for the meetings of the conference, but not easily surrendered, for two or three weeks, to any such use, without the probability of grave inconvenience to the archbishop's household. I ventured to say so; whereupon the archbishop promptly replied, "Oh, they can't have it, if Mrs. Temple disapproves!" Mrs. Temple did disapprove, and we did n't have it!

It was this delightful candour on the part of Archbishop Temple which we Americans greatly admired, and envied. We had suffered at home from a bishop, at that time living, whose disease was a passion for insisting upon "points of order" in the sessions of the House of Bishops. His performances in the Lambeth Conference were a painful illustration of the maxim, "*Cœlum, non animum, mutant, qui trans mare currunt*," and, in the Lambeth Conference, he was perpetually on his feet, stating points of order. At last, one morning, the

patience of one of the Anglican prelates having been exhausted, he rose and made a
protest, to the effect that the American Bishop
———, who had spoken six times that morning,
so making it impossible for the Bishop of ———
to speak at all, was "out of order." There
was a pause and then the sharp voice of the
primate was heard, saying, "Oh, yes ; he is
grossly out of order. But I have no doubt
that he is ashamed of it, by this time." It is
hardly necessary to say that we heard no more
from the American Bishop of ———.

Indeed, the primate was a terror to bores.
Near where some of the junior American
bishops sat, was a British colonial bishop who,
because he had a fashion of sitting with his
foot curled up beneath him, and springing suddenly to his feet that he might interject into
the debates, at intervals all too brief, remarks
that were of no pertinence and no value, was
profanely called "the kangaroo." One day
when Archbishop Temple, who was nearly
blind, was leaning on my arm on his way out
of the library, we met this colonial bishop.
' B———," said the archbishop, calling him, *more
Anglicano*, by the name of his diocese, "are n't
you tired?" "No, your Grace," said the
bishop, evidently perplexed by the question,

" I am not tired." " You ought to be ! " said the archbishop in his most rasping tones, and that bishop was heard from no more.

Archbishop Temple suffered, during his later years, from some affection of the eyes which made it often impossible for him to recognise those who spoke to him. But his kindness of heart was unfailing, and it led him into some curious blunders. An English clergyman told me that, on one occasion, at a garden party at Lambeth, when his guests were paying their respects to him, he said to one of those who approached him, " How do you do ?   How is your father ? "

The guest looked somewhat surprised, and said, " My father is dead, your Grace."

" And the widow, your mother, how is she?" said the archbishop.   " Thank you," said the guest a little stiffly, "she is quite well."

As he passed on, the archbishop turned to a clergyman who stood near him and said, "By the way, who was that ? "   Said the archdeacon who answered the question, I am afraid with a little spice of mischief in his tone, " That, your Grace, was the Duke of Connaught."

But in spite of his eccentricities of temper and of speech, England has not often seen a greater archbishop than Temple.   Men have said that the English Church has blundered in turning, so often, to the public schools for her bishops. Think of it! Every one of those whom I have recalled here had been a master, or head master, at Rugby. I have not myself the smallest doubt that, in governing boys, they learned how to govern men; and that, in that microcosm of the larger life of dioceses and provinces, they were trained with pre-eminent fitness and thoroughness for the greater tasks of the archiepiscopate. "All life," we are wont to say, "is a schoolroom." Happy he who can take with him into the arenas of the greater world the lessons that he has learned as a boy!

FINIS.